Unidimensional Scaling of Social Variables

Unidimensional Scaling of Social Variables
Concepts and Procedures

Raymond L. Gorden

THE FREE PRESS
A Division of Macmillan Publishing Co., Inc.
NEW YORK

Collier Macmillan Publishers
LONDON

The Free Press
A Division of Macmillan Publishing Co., Inc.
866 Third Avenue, New York, N.Y. 10022

Collier Macmillan Canada, Ltd.

Library of Congress Catalog Card Number: 76-26443

Printed in the United States of America

printing number

1 2 3 4 5 6 7 8 9 10

Library of Congress Cataloging in Publication Data

Gorden, Raymond L
    Unidimensional scaling of social variables.

    Bibliography: p.
    Includes index.
    1. Scaling (Social sciences) I. Title.
H61.G57   300'.1'51   76-26443
ISBN 0-02-912580-4

The scale on page 7, from Paul Wallin's "A Guttman
Scale for Measuring Women's Neighborliness," AJS 59
(Nov. 1953):243, is reproduced by permission of the
copyright holder, The University of Chicago Press.

Contents

List of Figures

Preface

This book is intended both for the novice with no theoretical background in scaling and for the person with a background in concepts who discovers missing links when he attempts to apply these concepts to concrete problems.

During several years of teaching scaling, I have discovered that only rarely is a student able to develop his own unidimensional scale after reading the available, scattered technical materials on scaling. This is usually because of two serious omissions in the literature. First, it deals mostly with the theoretical concepts and mathematical bases of scaling while neglecting to show how to *discover* or *construct* a set of verbal items for a questionnaire which have a high probability of proving to be unidimensional. Typically, the student chooses items, uses them in their raw form, administers the questionnaire, applies a test of unidimensionality, and finds that the items do not even approximate a scale. Furthermore, he or she may fail to get any clues from the data as to why the set was not scalable.

A second serious gap in the literature is the failure to spell out the concrete operations clearly, particularly for items with more than a dichotomous response pattern. Much of the literature implies that the same concepts that are illustrated with dichotomous items can also be applied to items with three, four, or five possible answers. Yet the needed procedures are not illustrated, and the reader is not warned of the complications that might result.

To remedy these gaps I have presented a step-by-step explanation beginning with a discussion of the applicability of scaling methods to the measurement of social forces, social processes, and social structures. Then I show the basic logico-mathematical forms of scales and indicate which are applicable to measuring social variables. A condensed review is supplied of the continuities in the development of the scaling of social attitudes, from the Bogardus single-item Social Distance scale to the unidimensional set of scale items as developed by Guttman.

The book deals extensively with the strategies and techniques of discovering, selecting, and constructing attitude items and emphasizes building in the calibration at three levels: the selection of *content themes*, the construction of *facet types*, and the construction of *response forms*. A thorough understanding of these concepts and their attendant operations will greatly increase the probability of developing a questionnaire that will prove to be unidimensional according to the rigorous Guttman criteria.

In explaining the operations for testing and diagnosing unidimensionality, I present a procedure that can be followed without any scalogram board, without a computer, without any equipment or materials other than the Scalogram Sheet included in Appendix A. The simple scalogram-sheet method allows the use of items with two to five answer categories; it can be used with small samples of cases (from 10 to 30) without requiring large-scale field work, which makes it practical for the learner; and it produces a visual pattern on the scalogram that closely approximates the logical concept of scaling.

To unite concepts, insights, operations, and skills, I have developed a series of eight laboratory problems that develop a step-by-step understanding of the full range of operations, from discovering items to measuring and improving the coefficient of reproducibility.

Appendix A contains all the blank forms and other expendable materials needed to carry out the laboratory problems. The instructor or researcher may duplicate these forms. Appendix B contains the solutions to the laboratory problems.

I should like to acknowledge the help given by Dr. Lawrence Atherton in stimulating me to write this book and in discussing alternative modes of organizing and presenting the materials. My wife, Charlotte Gilson Gorden, has also made suggestions for improving the clarity of exposition and the readability; without her help the book would never have become a reality. The students in my Antioch College courses on Research Design and Field Methods helped in refining the laboratory problems.

R. L. G.
Yellow Springs, Ohio

Unidimensional Scaling of Social Variables

Chapter 1.   Scaling Theory

WHAT IS SCALING?

Scaling is essentially a method of measuring the amount of a property possessed by a class of objects or events. In the social sciences, "objects" include persons, groups, organizations, communities, and any other social entity. Social "events" include such a variety as marriages, robberies, elections, socialization, auto accidents, wars, riots, revolutions, and falling in love. The "properties" possessed by social objects or events may include such varied characteristics as truth, attitude, belief, solidarity, interdependence, self-sufficiency, hierarchy, happiness, success, or efficiency. To date, however, scaling has most often been used to measure the strength of an attitude or a belief possessed by individuals, and most of our illustrations will come from this area. In the future we can expect a continued wider application of scaling to deal with more properties and more social objects.

It is helpful to see scaling in relationship to the basic forms of quantification called *enumeration* and *measurement*. Enumeration consists of simply *counting* the number of *objects* (or events) of a certain class; measurement consists of specifying the *amount* of any clearly defined *property* possessed by an object or event. We can count concrete objects or events, but we cannot measure them. We can measure only a particular property (quality or dimension) of an object or event. This vital distinction between enumeration and measurement is often blurred in common parlance; we say "he measured the stick" when we actually mean "he measured the length of the stick." He could also have measured the width, diameter, weight, hardness, tensile strength, carbon content, or many other properties possessed by the stick.

The importance of the distinction between enumeration and measurement becomes clear when we encounter the vast difference be-

1

tween establishing the method, procedure, reliability, and validity for *counting* the number of people in a small room and *measuring* each person's metabolism rate, body temperature, or attitude toward industrial pollution. Measuring involves *scaling*, which is a much more complex procedure than merely counting the number of objects or events of a certain class.

Obviously, enumeration and measurement share a common trait which puts them both in the general class of quantification. Both processes involve assigning a particular *magnitude* to our observations. This magnitude may be a precise number (as measured on a rate scale) or only an ordinal distinction that X is more than, equal to, or less than Y.

A less obvious, but equally important, characteristic shared by enumeration and measurement is that they both require prior *definition*. We cannot reliably quantify without first defining the objects or properties to be quantified.

In practice we often find that the apparently simple act of counting objects of a certain class may have low reliability (as indicated by the fact that two independent observers arrive at a very different count) unless careful attention is given to defining the class of objects we set out to count. For example, apparently simple questions like "How many families are now living in this city block?" or "How many schizophrenics are on Ward 9?" might be answered quite differently by two independent observers unless "family" and "schizophrenic" are clearly defined in operational terms.

The assumption that everyone knows what a family is can easily be proved to be quite imprecise when, for example, one census taker finds 15 families living in a block and another finds 19 in the same block on the same day. The image of the family as husband and wife with children living together in a house does not fit the complexities of the real world. How would we classify an unmarried woman with one child of her own who lives in a rooming house? Do the two constitute a family? Is a young widow with two children a family? If the widow and two children live with her mother, who is widowed but has two other children in college, how many families are there in that household? We discover that a complete and precise definition is needed to guide independent observers reliably to classify the same cases in the same categories.

It is even more obvious that the concept of "schizophrenic" would need a precise definition if independent observers were to agree on how many there are on Ward 9. In some mental hospitals patients might be classified as schizophrenic by a 5-to-7 vote of the professional staff. We cannot resolve this difficulty by saying that such a patient is 7/12 schizophrenic; we must clarify what we mean by schizophrenic and precisely what symptoms can be depended upon as indicators of schizophrenia.

The fact that both enumeration and measurement must involve the preliminary step of definition helps to clarify the confusion often promoted by the false dichotomy between qualitative studies and quantitative studies. Often this confusion is caused by the assumption that if one is doing a quantitative study one need not be concerned with any qualitative aspect of the phenomenon under inspection. Nothing could be further from the truth. Although it is correct to say that to do a qualitative study you need not concern yourself with an quantification, the reverse of this statement is not true. In studying social phenomena, just as in studying chemistry, we must know how to do qualitative analysis before doing quantitative analysis.

Whether we are in the physical, biological, or social sciences, we may find that, even though we clearly define the object or property to be observed and quantified, we cannot directly *observe* what we want to count or measure. In physics we cannot actually see an atom, but we can see the effects of an atom. In biology we cannot actually see a virus with the naked eye, and in social psychology we cannot actually see an attitude or belief, but we can see their effects as they are expressed in overt behavior of some kind. Similarly, we cannot see the unconscious mind, yet it is possible to see its effects in a demonstration of post-hypnotic suggestion.

This indirectness of observation seems to be more generally associated with the measurement operation than with counting. Even the most common measurements of physical phenomena usually depend upon some special instrument which transforms the units of the quality we want to measure into units of linear space, which we can see directly. This can give us the false impression that, for example, when we look at a thermometer, we are "seeing the temperature." This is no more correct than to think that when we look at a person's attitude-scale score we are "seeing his attitude." Similarly, when we look at a speedometer, we do not see the speed of the car. When we look at a person's bank book, we are not seeing his wealth. In each case what we see is an indirect observation, an indicator that correlates with any fluctuations in the property we have defined for measurement.

It is this indirectness of most measurements that requires us to devise special operations and instruments which can be checked for reliability and validity.[1] Within this broader context of qualitative and

---

[1] The *reliability* of any observation, enumeration, or measurement is the probability that, if repeated at a later time by the same person, or at the same time by the same person, or at the same time by an independent competent observer,

quantitative analysis we use the word *scaling* to apply to all phases of measurement as opposed to enumeration. We define scaling as follows: *Scaling refers to the processes and techniques used to validate the existence of a defined property of an object or event and to establish operational indices of the relative magnitudes of the property.*

Unidimensional scaling theory and techniques focus on the problem of selecting a *set* of data items such as questions or observations that can be demonstrated to conform validly to a single social psychological dimension. The central concern is to determine which items belong in the set, to determine the ordinal position of the items on the scale, and to measure the validity of the scale in terms of some index of unidimensionality.

In contrast, multidimensional scaling tends to begin with a set of dimensions and focus attention on the problem of locating social objects in multidimensional space. In unidimensional scaling the object is described and compared with other objects in terms of their ordinal position on one dimension. In multidimensional scaling the object is described and compared with other objects in terms of their relative locations in multidimensional space.

USES OF UNIDIMENSIONAL SCALING IN THE SOCIAL SCIENCES

Whether discussing profound social issues or the most mundane events, we often tend to think in crude quantitative terms without realizing that the only way our statements could be empirically verified is by measuring with a scale. For example, an American says:

> When I toured Europe last summer I noticed that the Italians were much more tolerant of the Americans' attempts to speak Italian than the French were of the Americans' attempts to speak French. Also, those Americans who were abroad for the first time seemed more interested in their fellow Americans than were those who had been abroad many times before.

This statement implies two measurement scales. One might be called "Europeans' *tolerance* of foreigners' misuse of their language" and the other, "travelers' *interest* in fellow Americans met abroad." The accuracy of the statement could be verified only by devising two sets of questions, each constituting a scale corresponding to and measuring one of the two properties defined.

---

the observation will give the same result. The *validity* of an observation is the extent to which the concrete indicators correspond to the concept the researcher has defined. To ask "Is your observation valid?" means "Are you seeing, counting, or measuring what you think you are?"

The tendency to think in crude quantitative terms is universal in human behavior since all languages have words for better-worse, more-less, larger-smaller. In our society we do not hesitate to apply these words to properties of social as well as physical objects and events in our environment. Many false popular beliefs are perpetuated for decades because they are couched in vague quantitative terms which have never been put to the test of reality owing to the lack of any valid scale that could be used as the instrument of measurement.

For centuries men have been measuring the physical world with increasing sophistication. While the astronomers of Galileo's time were measuring the direction and speed of movement of the planets, and later, when the cartographers were finally getting an accurate measurement of the earth, its oceans and continents, no one was attempting to measure social properties such as social distance, group synergy, prejudice, empathy, or group solidarity.

We know that many ancient civilizations did count social events such as marriages, commercial transactions, or births, and social objects such as citizens, priests, or masons. But the gap between simple counting of events or objects and the measurement of significant properties of these events has proved to be a large one. This was not because people failed to observe these human properties, nor did they fail to notice that such properties as love, morale, loyalty, and hostility came in different strengths. What was lacking were the concepts and technology for constructing valid scaling instruments for social phenomena.

In the absence of the technical knowledge for handling the measurement operation, the consoling explanation was that it is impossible to "plumb the human heart," to "measure the imponderables of human behavior," or to "compare the mind of one man with another." The cry "it can't be done" was popular, yet the very persons raising the cry were constantly betrayed by their writings, which were full of propositions and assumptions regarding quantitative differences in social phenomena: statements such as, "the Macedonians are not as brave as their enemy," "my love for her has waned," or "the loyalty of the Trojan is greater than that of the Athenian." People insist on making quantitative statements as if the appropriate measurements have already been made. Perhaps we tend to avoid objective measurement, preferring to make judgments according to our own prejudices without interference from verifiable measures.

With the advent of social science we could no longer accept our "insightful sensitivity" as a reliable guide to ranking such social properties as marital success, neighborliness, or job satisfaction. The need for objective methods of measurement is demonstrated immediately when we see, for example, the amount of disagreement among self-appointed judges attempting to rank the same marriages as successful or unsuccessful. While public controversy tended to take extreme positions (for example, that marital success is a simple quality that can easily be judged and ranked or that it is an imponderable that cannot possibly be measured clearly and reliably), social scientists like Burgess and Wallin, in their classic studies of marriage,[2] were developing reliable and valid measures of marital success. In this effort they found they had to develop several different dimensions of "success" and that a particular marriage could be successful in one dimension and unsuccessful in another. Also, they found that the actual valid measurement of all the dimensions required hundreds of questions. The care taken in the design of the questions and the collection and analysis of the data provided a clear contrast to the crude, prescientific quantitative judgments made in everyday rhetoric. Although the complexity of the marital-success scales precludes their presentation here, we can illustrate a refined type of measurement of the concept of neighborliness devised according to the Guttman method by Paul Wallin.[3]

This neighborliness scale, presented on page 7, is a short, easy-to-administer scale used for investigating factors accounting for individual differences in neighborliness and for testing hypotheses as to intercommunity differences in neighborliness.

Since the beginning of the twentieth century there has been an accelerating growth in the development of measurement as distinct from enumeration in the study of man. The scaling of human properties has progressed from measurement of physiological traits (such as muscular strength, height, weight, and cephalic index) to measurement of psychological traits of individuals (such as visual acuity, speed of response, memory, judgment, intelligence). Scaling then progressed to measuring attitudes and beliefs of individuals and finally to properties of groups or interaction patterns among members of groups. There seems to have been an evolution in the development of the application of scaling from the physiological to the psychological, to the social-psychological, to the sociological, and finally to the social-anthropological.

BASIC APPLICATIONS OF SCALING

This book will focus mainly on the application of scaling to the measurement of social attitudes. However, there is no reason why

[2] Ernest W. Burgess and paul Wallin, *Engagement and Marriage* (Philadelphia: J. B. Lippincott Co.), 1953.

[3] Paul Wallin, "A Guttman Scale for Measuring Women's Neighborliness," *American Journal of Sociology* 59 (1953): 243–46.

A GUTTMAN SCALE FOR MEASURING
WOMEN'S NEIGHBORLINESS

(1) How many of your best friends who live in your neighborhood did you get to know since you or they moved into the neighborhood? Two or more (*GN*); one or none (*LN*).*

(2) Do you and any of your neighbors go to movies, picnics, or other things like that together? Often or sometimes (*GN*); rarely or never (*LN*).

(3) Do you and your neighbors entertain one another? Often or sometimes (*GN*); rarely or never (*LN*).

(4) If you were holding a party or tea for an out-of-town visitor, how many of your neighbors would you invite? Two or more (*GN*); one or none (*LN*)'

(5) How many of your neighbors have ever talked to you about their problems when they were worried or asked you for advice or help? One or more (*GN*); none (*LN*).

(6) How many of your neighbors' homes have you ever been in? Four or more (*GN*); three or less (*LN*).

(7) Do you and your neighbors exchange or borrow things from one another such as books, magazines, dishes, tools, recipes, preserves, or garden vegetables? Often, sometimes, or rarely (*GN*); never (*LN*).

(8) About how many of the people in your neighborhood would you recognize by sight if you saw them in a large crowd? About half or more (*GN*); a few or none (*LN*).

(9) With how many of your neighbors do you have a friendly talk fairly frequently? Two or more (*GN*); one or none (*LN*).

(10) About how many of the people in your neighborhood do you say "Hello" or "Good morning" to when you meet on the street? Six or more (*GN*); five or less (*LN*).

(11) How many of the names of the families in your neighborhood do you know? Four or more (2); one to three (1); none (0).†

(12) How often do you have a talk with any of your neighbors? Often or sometimes (*GN*); rarely or never (*LN*).

†(GN) means greater neighborliness and (LN) means less neighborliness.

†Responses to this question ended as a trichotomy in the scale. They can be scored as shown in the parentheses following the response categories.

scaling cannot also be used to measure individual action, interaction patterns, sequences of social action, structures of institutions, or any other social phenomenon. Basically, we might classify the hundreds of specific kinds of measurements of social properties into three categories: measurement of *forces*, description of *structures*, and description of *processes*.

Measurement of Forces

Attitude is considered a social-psychological force. This force influences but does not completely determine overt behavior because there are competing forces, such as anticipation of consequences and situational restraints, which prevent a simple direct expression of one's private attitude toward any social object.[4] In any situational analysis of interaction between people, we must take into consideration covert forces and counterforces that help to determine a person's overt behavior and also help the observer to interpret the meaning of an overt act. The human personality is a battleground of covert forces; basic physiological drives such as sex, hunger, or thirst compete with socially derived forces such as conscience, expectations, beliefs, faith, conscience, values, or attitudes. Such forces can potentially be measured by an appropriate scale.

Description of Structures

Insofar as any structure has a hierarchical arrangement, its parts comprise a scale. In the physical world some hierarchies are obvious and others are not. For example, it is clear that there is a hierarchy of dependence in the architecture of a building: the foundation supports the floor, the floor supports the walls, the walls support the roof. The *direction* of dependence is clear in that it is impossible to build a roof without walls, to build walls without a floor, or to build a floor without a foundation; yet it is possible to build a foundation without adding the floor and so on up the structure.

Social, political, and economic organizations similarly have structure. Of course not all structures are simple unidimensional hierarchies. Some of the elements may be ordered in a hierarchical fashion, and other elements which are functional parts may be interdependent but

---

[4] For example, see Raymond L. Gorden, "Interaction Between Attitude and the Definition of the Situation in the Expression of Opinion," *American Sociological Review* 17, No. 1 (1952): 50–58.

optional in their location. By Guttman scaling technique we can empirically discover which elements of a social structure or interaction pattern fall into a hierarchical arrangement. The Wallin scale for measuring women's neighborliness (page 7) is an example of a set of behavior items constituting a hierarchy of neighborliness.

Economic geographers have used this scaling concept to discover and demonstrate hierarchical patterns of economic interdependence among villages, towns, and cities. The specific elements in the structure vary with the level of economic development of a country. For example, such a scale pattern for Colombia would show that any town that did not have a drugstore would also lack an electrical repair shop, a hospital, and a university. Also, any town that did not have an electrical repair shop would not have a hospital, and any town without a hospital would also not have a university.

Sociologists have used Guttman scaling to demonstrate a number of hierarchical relationships. For example, Smith[5] used it for classifying urban neighborhoods according to the degree of demographic homogeneity. This scale demonstrates that in American cities of over 100,000 population there is a hierarchical relationship among such demographic factors as the proportion of males and females, the proportion of blacks and whites, and the proportion of the population under 21 years of age. Such a hierarchical arrangement is not a logical necessity but a product of social and historical forces. Similarly, certain scalable characteristics distinguish the sect, denomination, and ecclesia as types of religious institutions. Although Guttman scaling could be used in the search for such a hierarchy, many such studies do not use it.[6]

Political scientists have used Guttman scaling to detect patterns of voting in legislative bodies such as the United Nations General Assembly, city councils, state legislatures, and the Congress. They view these legislative bodies as groups structured according to scale-types of voting behavior of the members. McRae[7] has provided an example of the voting structure as revealed in a wide range of seemingly unrelated issues in 1948, including rent control, social security, public housing, the Taft-Hartley law, the National Science Foundation, the creation of the Department of Health, Education and Welfare, and

[5] Joel Smith, "A Method for the Classification of Areas on the Basis of Demographically Homogeneous Populations," *American Sociological Review* 19 (April, 1954): 201-207.

[6] For example, see Russell R. Dynes, "Church-Sect Typology and Socio-Economic Status," *American Sociological Review* 20 (October, 1955): 555-60.

[7] Ducan MacRae, Jr., *Dimensions of Congressional Voting* (Berkeley: University of California Press), 1958.

the control of Communists. This scale of behavior he called the Fair Deal scale.

Not only the behavior of legislators but also the behavior of Supreme Court justices has been scaled. A study by Schubert[8] showed that Supreme Court justices could be arranged in a reliable scale (coefficient of reproducibility .98) according to their willingness to accept a new trend in legislation rather than attempt to prove it unconstitutional.

It would be less than candid to fail to point out that there is considerable controversy among political scientists regarding the significance of scaling any political behavior patterns. However, the controversy can usually be settled by clarifying the purpose of the conditions under which scaling is meaningfully related to a basic problem. We must also take pains not to overinterpret the implications of such an empirical pattern.

Description of Processes

Here we use the term "process" simply to designate chronological stages or steps that repeatedly occur in some type of social change. In the empirical world there is often a close relationship between the chronological order of events and the hierarchy of interdependence among elements of a structure. Just as in the physical world the hierarchy of dependence in the architecture of a building determines the chronological steps in the construction process, we also find that in the social world there is often a direct relationship between structural hierarchy and process of change.

In some cases this strong relationship between hierarchy and process allows us to draw conclusions regarding the chronology of events without having to observe over a period of time. Thus a cross-sectional survey may be used as a substitute for a longitudinal survey. For example, we could draw statistically valid and reliable conclusions regarding the chronological order in which American households acquire major appliances by doing a sample survey of married couples in all age categories to find out which major appliances they have at the moment. If, for example, we found that everyone who had a television set also had a radio, that everyone with a freezer also had a refrigerator, that anyone with an electronic oven also had a freezer, and so on, we could demonstrate the order in which major appliances are usually acquired. If a family had only three major appliances, we

[8] Glendon Schubert, *Quantitative Analysis of Judicial Behavior* (Glencoe, Ill.: The Free Press, 1959).

would know (within statistical limits of the coefficient of reproducibility) which three they would be, or if they had nine, which nine they would be. From advertisers' point of view the practical implications of this knowledge are considerable. They could locate customers for electronic ovens, for example, by obtaining a list of people already owning freezers.

Not only do people tend to acquire material things in partially predictable order; institutions also tend to go through stages of growth and decay which seem to occur in cycles. For example, studies of Protestant religious groups find that there is a cycle of development from the *sect*, which is opposed to the religious establishment, to the *denomination*, which is in the process of accommodation with established religion and no longer in open conflict with the secular powers of business and government. The characteristics of recruitment of members and social structure of each type of group have been identified by Howard Becker.[9]

In an empirical study of religion, Liston Pope[10] goes further to explore the pattern of denominational development. He delineates 21 dimensions of organizational change involved in the process of development from a sect to a church. These dimensions include such changes as (a) from propertyless members to property owners, (b) from self-centered (personal) to culture-centered religion, (c) from suspicion of rival sects to disdain or pity for all sects, (d) from an unspecialized, unprofessional part-time ministry to a specialized, professional, full-time ministry, (e) from fervor in worship services to restrained listening, and (f) from stress on a future in the next world to primary interest in a future in this world.

Although Pope's study is mainly descriptive, exploratory, and impressionistic, it is a goldmine of suggestions of dimensions in the process of change that could be investigated using Guttman scaling as a tool to check the predictability (scalability) of steps within each dimension or to locate the basic dynamic underlying all the dimensions of structural change.

To illustrate the use of scaling to describe a social process, we will present a simplified version of a study of the behavior of U.S. Senators in voting for or against successive revised versions of a Congressional bill. If the sponsors of the bill make politically successful revisions of it, each successive revision should obtain more votes. To state this in another way, each successive version of the bill should

---

[9] Leopold von Wiese and Howard Becker, *Systematic Sociology* (New York: John Wiley & Sons, Inc., 1932), pp. 624–28.

[10] Liston Pope, *Millhands and Preachers* (New Haven: Yale University Press, 1942), pp. 117–40.

obtain "yes" votes from all Senators who had voted "yes" to a previous version and should also obtain "yes" votes from some of those who voted "no" on the previous version.

In Figure 1 we have organized simplified data to illustrate the effect of this hypothetically perfect strategy of revision. The column headings A, B, C, and D represent the successive revisions of the bill in chronological order. The sample of 15 Senators is arranged so that the names of those who voted "yes" on the most versions of the bill are on top of the list. Note that the number of "yes" votes ranges from 0 to 4, the maximum possible. By looking at the column totals we see that the number of "yes" votes on the original version of the bill was only 3. The second, third, and fourth versions of the bill received 7, 10, and 13 votes respectively. What makes this a perfectly scalable process is the fact in no case did a new revision lose a previous "yes" voter. Any "yes" vote picked up on a particular revision was retained through successive revisions. Of course this is not always

Figure 1. *Voting Behavior of Fifteen Senators on Four Versions of the Federal Aid to Higher Education Bill*

Senator	Number of "Yes" Votes on the Four Versions	Successive Versions of the Bill			
		A	B	C	D
Hill	4	Y	Y	Y	Y
Williams	4	Y	Y	Y	Y
Douglas	4	Y	Y	Y	Y
Hart	3	N	Y	Y	Y
Ervin	3	N	Y	Y	Y
Morse	3	N	Y	Y	Y
Bennett	3	N	Y	Y	Y
Nelson	2	N	N	Y	Y
Simpson	2	N	N	Y	Y
Anderson	2	N	N	Y	Y
Cotton	1	N	N	N	Y
Beall	1	N	N	N	Y
Cooper	1	N	N	N	Y
Scott	0	N	N	N	N
Smith	0	N	N	N	N
Total "Yes" Votes		3	7	10	13
Total "No" Votes		12	8	5	2

Source: Based on a study reported by William Buchanan, *Understanding Political Variables* (New York: Charles Scribner's Sons, 1969), pp. 185–89.

the way it happens in reality. But it would be possible to compare the effectiveness of the compromise revision process from one bill to another simply by measuring the proportions of votes that deviate from this perfectly scalable chronological pattern.

As we have tried to suggest with these few examples, if we have a clear understanding of the basic concepts of scaling as it applies to the construction of attitude scales, we will be able to apply the method to other areas of interest and other types of problems.

Two attempts to collect and evaluate some of the most frequently used sociological and psychological scales are the volumes by Bonjean and by Miller.[11] Bonjean catalogs the scales and indices alphabetically according to the property being measured (e.g., alienation, aspiration level, acculturation, authoritarianism, bureaucracy, centralization, class consciousness, cohesion, endogamy). Miller has collected 37 measuring instruments classified into the areas of (a) social status, (b) group structure and dynamics, (c) morale and job satisfaction, (d) community, (e) social participation, (f) leadership in the work organization, (g) attitudes, (h) family and marriage, and (i) personality. Here is a sample of the scales Miller describes in detail along with references to the studies in which they were used:

(1) Occupational Prestige Ratings (Hatt-North)
(2) Farm Socioeconomic Status Scale (Sewell)
(3) Group Cohesiveness Index (Seashore)
(4) Social Distance Scale (Bogardus)
(5) Scales of Military Base Morale (Guttman)
(6) Community Solidarity Index (Fessler)
(7) Scale for Measuring Women's Neighborliness (Guttman)
(8) Social Insight Scale (Chapin)
(9) Willingness to Tolerate Conformity (Stouffer)
(10) Marriage Prediction Schedule (Burgess)

Although hundreds of scales have been devised covering many aspects of human behavior, there is an increasing need to devise new scales to fit the particular focus in which we are interested. Also, many of the existing scales are culture-bound and must be adapted and revalidated when used in a different culture or subculture.

There have been some notable attempts to devise scales which are polycultural from the beginning. For example, the OM Scale was devised to measure the "overall modernity" of a person's values by

---

[11] Charles M. Bonjean *et al., Sociological Measurement: An Inventory of Scales and Indices* (San Francisco: Chandler Publishing Co., 1967). Delbert C. Miller, *Handbook of Research Design and Social Measurement* (New York: David McKay Co., 1964). Part III presents "Selected Sociometric Scales and Indices".

including values associated with the rural agrarian life at one end of the scale and values associated with the urban industrial life at the other end.[12] Beginning with hundreds of questions translated into about a dozen languages, the researchers gradually eliminated those that did not have a constant cross-cultural meaning and finally developed a set of 14 items which has proved to be a unidimensional scale in cultures as diverse as the United States, Korea, and Germany.

Many scales were initially designed to be used in one country and were found to be indadequate when applied in another. For example, Dodd[13] describes the changes that had to be made in order to apply the Bogardus Social Distance Scale in the Near East, particularly with respect to Arabs' attitudes toward Jews even in 1935!

Not only must existing scales be adapted to other cultures or subcultures, but also the specific wording of items on a particular topic must be periodically updated to fit new historical circumstances and new usage. For example, statements that were meaningful to American middle-class teenagers in 1972 may not be meaningful in 1978.

The point is that the time will never arrive when we in the social sciences will *not* have to know how to design and validate new scales since old ones constantly need to be adapted and revalidated to accommodate historical changes in the culture or to fit the requirements of cross-cultural comparison.

Another source of increasing demand is the requirement by many governmental and private agencies that program evaluations be performed which often should include some type of measurement scale. Also, the variety of problems attacked by social scientists and social practitioners is expanding at an accelerating rate.

In order to provide the reader with a clear understanding of both the theory and the practical application of scaling, we will avoid the unnecessary confusion and complexity that would be introduced if we attempted to deal with the measurement of social forces, social hierarchies, and social processes in the same book, concentrating on the application of scaling to the measurement of one type of social force, called attitude. Once this is thoroughly understood, there is no difficulty in applying the theory and procedures to the scaling of any type of social or psychological variable.

So far we have defined scaling as a process of measurement of properties of objects as distinct from the enumeration of the objects themselves. The tendency for people to talk about human relations

---

[12] D. H. Smith and Alex Inkeles, "The OM Scale: A Comparative Socio-Psychological Measure of Individual Modernity," *Sociometry* 29, No. 4 (December, 1966): 353-77.

[13] Stuart C. Dodd, "A Social Distance Test in the Near East, *American Journal of Sociology* 41 (September, 1935): 194-204.

and personal characteristics in crude measurement terms is as old as human society itself. Only in recent history has social science evolved more valid, reliable, precise, and sophisticated methods of measurement. We have shown that social-psychological forces, social structures or patterns, and processes of social change are all susceptible to measurement and, therefore, involve the process of scaling.

BASIC MATHEMATICAL TYPES OF SCALES

In order to go beyond a definition of scaling and an explanation of why it is needed to discover how we can actively engage in the creative process of scale building, we must first understand some of the most essential mathematical properties of scales. In this section we will describe the basic mathematical models of the scale. The remainder of the book deals with the empirical procedures for determining the fit between social reality and one of the mathematical models. Understanding these mathematical models is not difficult and has benefits far beyond the problem of scale building, because the type of scale used determines the operations (logical, mathematical, and statistical) that can be used legitimately in drawing conclusions from the data.

Scales can be classified according to their logico-mathematical properties. All scales share the property of dimensionality. That is to say, we must know that whatever qualitative or quantitative categories we designate in the scale do in fact constitute a single dimension. In addition to this *sine qua non* a scale may have certain mathematical features and refinements. With each added feature we increase the number and variety of analytic models that can be used in describing the distribution of the measurements of a single characteristic and in analyzing relationships among different characteristics. The basic types of scales we will describe are: *nominal*, *ordinal*, *interval*, and *ratio*.

The Nominal Scale

The adjective "nominal" means "in name only." The nominal scale is called a scale because it has the most essential property common to all types of scales: dimensionality. Yet it is not really a scale because it lacks the other essential characteristic of measurement, which is calibration. Let's look at its property of dimensionality.

A dimension represents a concept that is capable of being divided logically into subclassifications. In general, the subclassifications may represent either qualitative or quantitative differences among objects falling into the general conceptual dimension. When the differences are only qualitative but are clearly subcategories of the larger concept, then this set of subcategories constitutes a nominal scale.

For example, the concept "sex" has two subcategories. If we have defined it in purely biological terms, then the subcategories are called male and female; if we define sex in sociological terms of the roles, values, or attitudes associated with the biological types, then we might want to call the two subcategories "masculine" and "feminine." In either case the concept, or dimension, has two subcategories.

Standard statistical terminology refers to nonquantitative divisions of the dimension as *categories* in contrast to *class intervals*, which refers to quantitative divisions. Many social characteristics, because of their very nature, must be represented by a nominal scale, and any attempt to force the data into the form of a calibrated scale would be a distortion of reality. For example, the dimension of "political affiliation" might be represented by the subcategories of Democrat, Republican, and Other. In classifying the registered voters of a particular county into a three-category table, there is no quantitative rationale to indicate that the category "Democrat" should be to the left (lower) or to the right (higher) than "Republican." We must not be confused by the fact that in general Democrats might be slightly to the "left" of Republicans in political attitudes. The commonly used political attitude dimension (reactionary, conservative, liberal, radical) is not the same dimension as political affiliation. The former can be calibrated and the latter cannot.

Assigning such significance to the nominal scale may seem to overemphasize an elementary point. Yet, in the history of scaling in the social sciences, we have found that failure to recognize the basic importance of dimensionality has led to a premature preoccupation with refining the calibration *before* it has been established that the numbers used actually refer to the same dimension. Often a total score obtained by adding the values of the responses to several questions in an attitude scale is the logical equivalent of weighing oranges and apples together when trying to obtain the weight of the oranges only.

The Ordinal Scale

The *ordinal scale* builds logically upon the nominal scale by adding the property of *rank* to that of *dimensionality*. In the ordinal scale we know not only that the attributes we have named are subcategories of a single larger characteristic but also that these subcategories belong in a certain *rank order* because they represent different amounts of the characteristic. For example, it is obvious that small, medium, and large belong in a rank order with medium in the middle. Similarly, it is obvious that those who finish in first, second, and third places in a race fall into a rank order with regard to their speed. Now we have introduced a quantitative property in relating the subcategories to each other within the qualitative dimension.

Sometimes ordinal quantification is called *comparison*, in contrast to *measurement*. Regardless of the terminology used, the important point is that we can know that an object is longer, heavier, or harder than another object, or that a person is funnier, happier, or healthier than another person, without knowing *how much* longer or how much happier. Such knowledge is useful for many purposes as long as we can demonstrate that the objects or persons can be reliably classified into these ordinal categories.

The Interval Scale

The intervale scale adds the property of *distance* to those of *dimensionality* and *rank*. In the interval scale we know not only that the categories belong on a single dimension and in a certain rank order; we also know how far it is between one point and another on the scale. For example, if we establish a scale in which degrees of hardness are represented by points from 1 to 10, and if we can demonstrate that amount of difference in hardness between 1 and 2 is the same as that between 2 and 3, 3 and 4, 4 and 5, etc., then we have an interval scale. In other words, we have a scale in which all the intervals are equal. It is easy to demonstrate that the one-inch intervals on a precise ruler are actually equal intervals in terms of linear units, but it is a more complex problem to discover whether the distance between 100 and 101 degrees Farenheit is equal to the interval between 200 and 201 degrees in terms of thermal units. We must not deceive ourselves into thinking that these two problems are basically the same merely because the thermometer scale, like the ruler, is in terms of linear units. In the case of the ruler the units on the scale are actually linear units, and the ruler is measuring linear distance; but in the case of the thermometer, the scale is in terms of linear units which we assume to *represent* or to *correlate with* thermal units. In the first case the measurement is direct; in the second case it is indirect. Even though most measurement in the physical, biological, or social sciences is of the indirect sort, we attempt to represent the quantities involved by translating the original dimension into linear distance.

Obviously the interval scale is superior to the ordinal scale since the former tells us everything the latter does and more. If we measure with an interval scale, these measurements can be translated validly into ordinal measures or ranks; but if we measure with an ordinal scale, there is no way we can translate the ordinal measurements into interval measurements. For example, if we measure ten children and obtain their exact height in inches, we can validly translate these measurements into rank order of height represented by numbers from 1 to 10. But if we had merely arranged these same ten children in line by height and assigned the same rank numbers to them without ever having measured them with a ruler, we could not validly translate the children's rank order into a specific height in inches.

The interval-scale information is also superior because it it possible to add the individual heights of the ten children and obtain the total height or the mean height of all the children in the group of ten. Furthermore, if we wanted to compare the average height of a sample of children in a California school with that of children in a New York school, it would be impossible to make such a comparison without an interval scale.

The Ratio Scale

Although the interval scale is superior to the ordinal scale, it does not have all of the desirable properties of measurement. It lacks a point of *natural origin*, known as the zero point on the scale. The *ratio scale* adds this fourth property. If the scale does not have a natural origin which fixes the location of the zero point on the scale, or if we assume that we can move the zero point arbitrarily, or if the location of zero is unknown, then we cannot use the measurements as ratios in mathematical manipulations.

For example, suppose that we had two yardsticks, each 36 inches long, and each accurate in the sense that all of the one-inch intervals were equal, but we assume that the location of the zero point (which mathematically divides the negative numbers from the positive numbers) is purely arbitrary. We assume that the zero on yardstick A is at the extreme end, as usual, but on yardstick B it is 10 inches from the end. This is the case in Figure 2.

We then use these two yardsticks to measure two objects. According to the first yardstick object A is 11 inches long and object B is

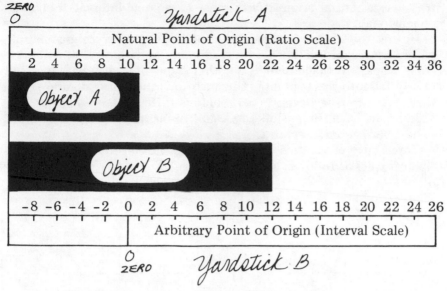

Figure 2. *Ratio Scale versus Interval Scale*

22 inches long. Therefore, object B is twice as long as object A. That is, the *ratio* of the length of B to A is 2:1. According to the second yardstick, the lengths of objects A and B are 1 inch and 12 inches; therefore, it might appear that object B is 12 times as long as object A. Yet the actual length of neither object has changed. We cannot validly obtain a ratio by dividing one measurement by the other if there is not a natural (as opposed to an artificial or arbitrary) point of origin which determines the location of the zero on the scale.[14]

Ordinal Plus Natural Origin

The fourfold typology of scales according to their basic properties has been a standard point of view for decades and is a useful conceptualization of scales. This typology assumes that the properties of *dimensionality*, *rank order*, *equal intervals*, and *natural origin* are in themselves a chronological sequence or heirarchy. Therefore, if a

[14] Note that the arbitrary location of movement of the zero point does not invalidate a comparison of the lengths of objects A and B by *subtraction*. The difference between the lengths of objects A and B using either ruler is 11 inches. Since we can compare by either division or subtraction when using the *ratio* scale, we can say that from the mathematical point of view, the ratio scale is superior to the interval scale as well as to the ordinal and nominal scales.

scale has a natural origin it also must have equal intervals, rank, and dimensionality.

However, with the increasing use of the Guttman scaling method, which has been developed empirically and systematically, it has become apparent that there is another type of scale that does not clearly fall into this typology. Guttman and others have demonstrated that scales can be devised, particularly in the measurement of attitudes, that have dimensionality, rank order, and natural origin but do *not* have equal intervals.

Torgeson[15] points this out and suggests another fourfold classification of scales as follows:

		Natural Origin	
		Yes	*No*
Equal Intervals	*Yes*	Ratio	Interval
	No	Ordinal (nat. org.)	Ordinal (no nat. org.)

Thus he drops the nominal scale of the more traditional scheme and adds a new type, which he calls the ordinal-scale-with-natural-origin.

A Revised Typology

We feel that it is an improvement to add the new type but that the nominal-scale category should be retained and understood as the most rudimentary form representing the basic property of dimensionality common to all types of scales. It is precisely this property of dimensionality that distinguishes a set of categories that makes up a scale from all other sets.

Guttman has demonstrated that in the construction of attitude scales we can locate the zero point on the scale even when we have not established that the intervals are equal. The zero point is the midpoint between the least pro and the least anti statements. This is also the point at which the intensity of feeling is minimal. It has been shown that people who score on either extremes of the scale have the

[15] Warren S. Togerson, *Theory and Methods of Scaling* (New York: John Wiley & Sons, Inc., 1958), pp. 15-17.

strongest feelings and that these feelings approach zero as we move inward toward the neutral point in the scale, as shown in Figure 3.

In order to allow for the ordinal scale with a natural origin and at the same time retain the nominal scale within the same scheme, we propose a revised typology of scales as shown in Figure 4. Although adding the third type of scale may offend by disturbing an otherwise neat pattern of Xs, this revised typology more nearly describes the full range of reality in the scaling of social-psychological variables.

SCALES AND STATISTICAL MEASURE

Although our main purpose is to describe and explain scaling concepts and procedures, we should like to show quickly how the type

Figure 3. *Intensity and the Zero Point*

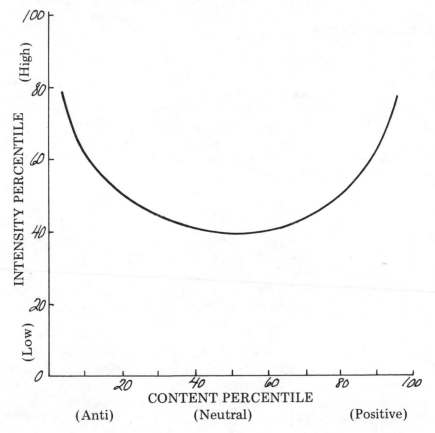

TYPE OF SCALE	PROPERTIES			
	Dimen-sion	Order	Distance	Origin
1. Nominal	X			
2. Ordinal	X	X		
3. Ordinal + origin	X	X		X
4. Interval	X	X	X	
5. Ratio	X	X	X	X

Figure 4. *Types of Scales and Their Properties*

of scale used in the original measurement determines the type of analysis that can be applied to the resulting data. We will discuss only the most commonly used statistical measures of *central tendency*, *dispersion*, and *association* as they relate to the type of scale used.

Nominal-Scale Data

Central Tendency.   The categories in a nominal scale have no natural order of magnitude, and they cannot be represented by numbers, either ordinal or cardinal. Therefore, we cannot represent the whole distribution in all the categories by any type of single number. Instead, we can describe the central tendency by simply saying which category has the most cases in it, what proportion of all the cases fall into this one category, and what proportion of all the cases fall into each category. For example:

Religion	f	Percentage
Catholic	25	50%
Protestant	15	30
Jewish	8	16
Buddhist	2	4
Totals	50	100%

Since these are nonquantitative categories (usually called attributes) it is meaningless to ask, "What was the average religion of the sample of 50 people interviewed?" We can say, "Most were Catholic" or, more precisely, "50% were Catholic," but we cannot give a simple one-figure numerical answer which corresponds to a mean or median value. In effect we are giving the mode by naming the modal category. Certainly the answer would be very different for a sample from Kamakura, where the modal category would be Buddhist rather than Catholic. But if we were comparing a sample from Boston with a sample from Dublin, we would find that the central tendency in both distributions would be Catholic. In order to show the differences in the central tendencies of the two distirbutions, we would have to show what percent of the total fell into the modal category in each case.

Thus, with a nominal scale we can represent the central tendency of the distribution by naming the modal category and showing the percentage falling in that category. This allows us to compare the central tendency of one distribution with that of another on the same nominal scale.

Dispersion. Of course, knowing the percentage of cases that fall into the modal category does not tell us what percentages fall into the rest of the categories in the distribution unless there are only two categories. With the nominal scale all we can do is show what percent of the total number of cases falls into each of the categories. This allows us to compare one pattern of dispersion with another on the same nominal scale.

Association. If we want to obtain a measure of the amount of association between one nominal scale and another, we are engaging in measuring *contingency* in contrast to *correlation*, which applies only to quantitative categories derived from ordinal, interval, or ratio scale data. For example, if we want to know whether there is a strong association between a voter's race and his political party affiliation we could display the association between the two nominal-scale characteristics simply by making up a two-dimensional table with two rows labeled "black" and "white" and two columns labeled "Democrat" and "Republican." Then the four cells could be filled in to show how many blacks are Democrats and how many Republicans, and how many whites are Democrats and how many Republicans. In order to *measure* the strength of the association between race and party in this particular table we would have to apply statistical measures of contingency such as T^2 (Tschuprow's T), C (coefficient of contingency), and others which are explained in standard statistics texts.

Ordinal-Scale Data

Since the ordinal scale has dimensionality plus magnitude, we can use all the same measures of central tendency, dispersion, and association used with nominal-scale data *plus* the additional statistical measures indicated below.

Central Tendency. When we have a distribution of measurements on an ordinal scale, we can show the central tendency simply by specifying the median value or score. The median is that point on the scale above which 50% of the distribution is found and below which the remaining 50% of the distribution is found.

Dispersion. The interquartile range is a standard way of showing the dispersion of ordinal measurements. This figure simple tells us the two points on the ordinal scale between which not only the median falls but also 50% of the total distribution. Another way of defining the interquartile range is that it is that range which includes the second and third quartiles of any distribution. Two distributions on the ordinal scale which have the same median value may have very different distributions on either side of the median. This would be reflected in the differences between the interquartile ranges, or in the comparisons of quartiles.

Association. The most commonly used measure of association between two ordinal variables is the Spearman Rank Correlation (*Rho*). This is a single figure which ranges from -1 for perfect negative correlation to +1 for perfect positive correlation. The calculations are fairly simple to do with no equipment other than an adding machine and a table of squares if the number of cases is small (for example, from 10 to 20). It is possible to obtain statistically significant rank correlations with as few as five cases. Rank correlations can be done very rapidly for up to 1,000 cases using electronic data-processing equipment.

An important consideration in constructing a unidimensional ordinal scale is to have a large range of possible total scores (for example 0–80 rather than 0–10) so that in doing rank correlations there will not be many cases in which two or more people have the same score. For example, if we work with a sample of 20 people and have a scale range of only 10 points, we know in advance that there will be either ten cases where two people have the same score or fewer cases where three or more people have the same score. In either case the mathematical requirements for the rank correlation are violated.

This is the reason that we find many studies in which scale scores are obtained to be correlated with another set of scale scores, and the rank correlation is not used. To salvage the operation the investigator converts the ranked scores into the quantitative categories of "high," "medium," and "low." This allows the amount of association to be measured by Tschuprow's T^2 or some other measure of contingency. This procedure has the disadvantage that a larger number of cases is required to obtain a degree of association which would be statistically significant.

Ordinal Scale with Natural Origin

All the measures applicable to the ordinal data without a natural origin also apply in cases where there is a natural origin to the scale.

Interval-Scale and Ratio-Scale Data

Central tendency: In addition to the *mode* and *median* we may validly calculate an *arithmetic mean* from the distribution on either an interval or a ratio scale. The fact that the equality of intervals corresponds to the mathematical assumption that the distances between intergers are equal allows us to add the values to obtain the mean. Of course, in the case of the interval scale, if we move the zero point, we will naturally obtain a different value for the mean of the distribution, but for reasons explained below this would not change the measure of dispersion as measured by the *standard deviation*.

Dispersion.   The appropriate measure of dispersion for distributions based on either the interval or the ratio scale is the *standard deviation*. The lack of a natural zero does not hamper this operation since *deviation* is measured from the mean of the distribution regardless of what value is assigned to the mean point. Also, whether the difference (mean minus the value of a particular case in the distribution) is negative or positive does not matter since the standard deviation is the square root of the sum of the squared differences divided by the total number of cases. In squaring all values become positive.

Association.   Since the formula for the Pearson Product Moment correlation is based upon the standard deviation as a unit of measurement, we can use the Pearsonian correlation with data measured by either an interval or a ratio scale, assuming that the other requirements regarding the shape of the distribution are met.

The relationship between the type of scale data and the permissible statistical measures is summarized in Figure 5, which includes the most commonly used statistical measures in each of the three categories.[16]

Unidimensional *vs.* Multidimensional Scaling

Although this book focuses on unidimensional scaling, it might be helpful to show its relationship to multidimensional scaling and the conditions under which unidimensional scaling is a necessary step to multidimensional scaling.

[16] Dean J. Champion, *Basic Statistics for Social Research* (Scranton, Pa.: Chandler Publishing Co., 1970).

SCALE TYPE	Statistical Measures Permissible		
	Central Tendency	Dispersion	Association
Nominal	Name the modal category	Percentage distribution	Contingency (X^2, T^2, Q, etc.)
Ordinal*	Modal value Median value	Above plus interquartile range	Above plus rank correlation (Rho)
Interval and Ratio	Mode Median Mean	Above plus Standard Deviation	Above plus Pearsonian r

*With or without a natural point of origin or zero point.

Figure 5. *Statistical Measures Permissible by Scale Type*

Unidimensional scaling theory and techniques are aimed at selecting a set of data items (questions, observations, etc.) that can be empirically demonstrated to correspond to a single social-psychological dimension. The whole focus is to obtain a fit between the empirical world of reality and the conceptual world of logical definitions. This is a two-way process. The procedure can be used either to *test* the proposition that a particular concept corresponds to a certain quantitative property of reality or, in an exploratory way, to *discover* the existence of certain quantitative properties.

Multidimensional scaling, on the other hand, emphasizes the concepts and procedures for locating any social object (whether an individual, a group, an event, an activity, a process, an institution, or a social system) in multidimensional space. Instead of simply measuring the amount of a particular property of an object, the problem is simultaneously to classify the object according to two or more properties. Only some of the hundreds of properties of the object are selected for analysis in a multidimensional table. In this case the "object" corresponds to a physical body which "contains" certain physical and social properties. However, there is a different function of multidimensional scaling in situations where the "object" is by nature a multidimensional concept, defined strictly in terms of a multidimensional set of properties. Outside these properties it has no other proof of its existence. In this case the object by definition is represented by a certain location in property space. For example, suppose we define a *folk society* as a community with *definite geographical boundaries* in which the interacting people are *illiterate*, the division of labor pattern is so *simple* that 90% or more of the roles are determined by age and sex, a community which is *static* to the extent that all deviation from the traditions of the ancestors is taboo, and which is *small* enough that each adult knows who all the other adults are, either by name or by location in the kinship structure.

Armed with this definition, we could go about classifying societies in five-dimensional space as illustrated in Figure 6.

Since each of the five dimensions is dichotomous, there are 32 (2 to the 5th power) cells, or locations in multidimensional space. By definition the "folk society" is represented by one and only one of these 32 locations. The procedure could be used to classify many groups to discover which of them were folk societies or it could be used to discover whether there might be casual connections between one dimension and another. For example, after classifying many societies, we might find that cell Y was always empty. This might indicate that it is impossible for a society to be a large, complex, literate community and static at the same time. Or, if cell X was empty, this might mean that it is impossible for a society to be a small, simple, illiterate community and dynamic at the same time.

Logically, it may seem that all applications of multidimensional scaling would require the prior step of establishing the unidimensionality of each of the dimensions separately. How would we be justified in classifying an object according to several dimensions simultaneously if we had not first demonstrated that the indicators selected for dimension did in fact constitute the single-dimensioned concept? How would we even know that our dimension was indeed a conceptualization of something that existed in empirical reality?

Much of the treatment of multidimensional scaling seems to take the unidimensionality of each of the variables for granted and plunge immediately into the problem of locating a set of objects in multidimensional property space. Taking unidimensionality for granted is justifiable under two conditions: (1) if the quantification of the property is done by simple enumeration rather than by measurement and (2) if the properties represented by the dimensions are naturally dichotomous, all-or-none categories.

To illustrate the enumeration case, an urban census tract might be the object having the properties to be quantified, and the properties according to which it is to be classified might be size of population, density of housing, and crime rate. For each of these variables it is a conceptually simple matter to count the number of people, the number of houses per acre, or the number of crimes per 1,000 adult population. With simple enumeration there is no need to prove that 4,000 population is greater than 3,895, or that 12 dwelling units per acre is greater than four per acre.

Figure 6. *Five-Dimensional Classification of Societies*

	Community				Non-community			
	Literate		Illiterate		Literate		Illiterate	
	Static	Dynamic	Static	Dynamic	Static	Dynamic	Static	Dynamic
SIMPLE Small			FOLK SOCIETY	X				
Large								
COMPLEX Small								
Large	X							

Dichotomous properties are found to apply to many types of social objects. For example, census tracts may be inside or outside the city limits; they may be coincident with a previous township's or not, etc. Also, people fall into many dichotomous dimensions. For example, they are male or female, dead or alive, pregnant or not, single or married, parent or not. These are all nominal scales in which the unidimensionality of sex, life, pregnancy, marital status, and parenthood, respectively, can be safely accepted at face value.

None of these cases presents any problem of scaling as such. Both counting of people as a variable property of census tracts called population and putting people into all-or-none categories according to certain dichotomous properties they possess are examples of types of enumeration rather than of scaling. Therefore, this type of cross-classification of objects does not involve scaling in the strict sense even though it often is labeled "multidimensional scaling."

However, there are other examples of multidimensional scaling which do indeed involve measurement in contrast to mere enumeration. Sometimes, the users of multidimensional scaling techniques, even when dealing with scalable properties, simply take the unidimensionality for granted. This is more likely to happen when the researcher treats ordinal variables *as if* they were dichotomous by merely dividing the distribution into "high" and "low," either at the middle of the scale or at the middle (mode, mean, or median) of the distribution. This might be done for simplicity or convenience. When the number of cases is small sometimes the shape of the distribution necessitates such treatment in order to avoid violating certain assumptions in the statistical model used. When the number of cases is small, this is done in order to have large enough numbers in each class interval to assure an acceptable level of statistical significance. Such treatment involves some confusion because the artificial dichotomization of the distribution gives the outward appearance of a naturally dichotomous all-or-none property which did not exist in reality.

As an example, consider Max Weber's idea of Protestantism. Protestantism, as defined by Weber, is a multidimensional concept. We might take only two of the properties of Protestantism, reduce each of these to dichotomous categories, and represent the two-dimensional property space by a simple four-cell table, as shown in Figure 7. If the groups or individuals classified fall into the upper left-hand cell, they would be Protestant by definition. If none fell into the lower left or the upper right and some fell into the lower right, then we could suspect that there is some functional connection between asceticism and the emphasis on calling.

The important point here is that, in the foregoing example, scien-

		Emphasis on Asceticism	
		Yes	No
Emphasis on Calling	Yes	Prot.	?
	No	?	?

Figure 7. *Two-Dimensional Classification of Religion*

tific method demands that we first establish (1) that there is such a social reality as asceticism and (2) that the set of observations used as indicators of it do constitute a single dimension. This is necessary because these are not naturally dichotomous categories of a nominal scale. Obviously, people are not either ascetic or not. Some people may be more so than others, or the situations that call for asceticism in one culture may be different from the situations in another. Therefore, we are dealing with at least an ordinal scale.

We might ask, for example, is no asceticism the same as hedonism, or is it a neutral zero point halfway between asceticism and hedonism? How do we know that one person is more or less hedonistic than another? These questions can be settled only by the rigorous tests of unidimensionality. Once the unidimensionality of the scale items has been established, then we can decide where to dichotomize the distribution.

This process of classifying social objects in multidimensional property space, particularly when there are more than two dimensions, can be very fruitful either in testing hypotheses about functional relationships among the dimensions or as an exploratory device to determine which types of combinations exist in reality and which do not. Operationally, we can see which cells are occupied and which are still empty when our classification process is completed.

We have illustrated conditions under which multidimensional analysis need not be preceded by establishing unidimensionality and other conditions under which it must logically rest upon the prior establishment of unidimensionality. There are, of course, cases in which certain of the dimensions in a given multidimensional analysis need no proof of unidimensionality while others do. This would be the case, for example, if we simply substituted sex (male and female) for the "emphasis on calling" dimension of Figure 7.

Only in the cases where true measurement, rather than mere enumeration, is required must we deal with unidimensionality. We will trace the historical developments in unidimensional scaling leading up to the scaling technique developed by Louis Guttman.

THE DEVELOPMENT OF UNIDIMENSIONAL
SCALING IN THE SOCIAL SCIENCES

We pointed out earlier that man has been using quantitative data about his species since the ancient civilizations, when he counted the number of marriages, births, deaths, conversions, imprisonments, soldiers or taxpayers. Whenever he compiled any quantitative data, it was always in the form of enumerations, a result of counting people or human events, rather than measuring their social or psychological characteristics. Of course this did not inhibit man's tendency to make quantitative statements about social properties, such as "He is more friendly than the King," "She is more beautiful than most," "He is more intelligent than I," or "That city is more decadent than ours." Even though such quantitative statements can be found in the literature of ancient, medieval, and modern times, not until the twentieth century was any attempt made to measure any of these human properties objectively.

Here we will give only the briefest sketch of some of the high points of the development of measurement in the Untied States since World War I in order to put the Guttman scaling method, which is our ultimate concern, into a developmental perspective. If we were to list the persons who over the past 50 years have contributed to the development of measurement of human characteristics particularly relevant to the areas of sociology and social psychology in the United States, the following four names would have to appear: Emory S. Bogardus, Louis L. Thurstone, Rensis Likert, and Louis Guttman.

The Bogardus Social-Distance Scale

The concept of *social distance* has been a part of sociology since the turn of the century. Park[17] described it as "the grades and degrees of understanding and intimacy which characterize pre-social and social relations generally." The concepts of "ingroup-outgroup" in sociology, of "acceptance-rejection" in psychology, of "ethnocentricism" in anthropology, all relate to the general idea of social distance. Park never attempted to measure social distance systematically, but his interest in race relations made the concept central to him.

In the 1920s Emory Bogardus began to develop measures of social distance. His *Immigration and Race Attitudes*, published in 1929,

[17] Robert E. Park, "The Concept of Social Distance," *Journal of Applied Sociology* 8 (1902), 339–44.

applied a scale to measure the social distance between a random sample of native Americans and each of several immigrant gorups.[18] Later, in 1956, he measured the social distance of 2,953 selected persons throughout the United States from 30 different racial or ethnic groups. The most complete treatment of the Bogardus Social-Distance Scale was published in 1959.[19]

His procedure was simple, as is shown in Figure 8, a sample excerpt from the social-distance questionnaire. Bogardus simply assumed (correctly in most cases) that the seven responses, ranging from admitting the person to close kinship by marriage to excluding the person from the United States, represented ordinal points on a unidimensional scale. Even though the assumption of unidimensionality and the order of the items were not empirically tested, the scale was probably very reliable in ranking the different ethnic groups according to social distance within the general cultural framework of the United States. This could happen because (a) the seven items do correspond with different degrees of social intimacy, with which Bogardus was acquainted both as a sociologist and a member of American society; and (b) more important, probably, since social intimacy does correlate empirically with physical proximity and probable frequency of interaction, the empathic face value of the items in the mind of the researcher corresponded very closely with the meaning for the respondents to the scale. It would have been very easy to test the unidimensionality of these seven items simply by looking at the pattern of responses of individuals to a given racial group. Since the instructions say, "Put a cross after each race in as many of the seven rows as your feeling dictates," then each respondent will give a *pattern* of responses for every race listed. These patterns will show as either scalable or not.[20]

Example A—Scalable Pattern Response Categories								*Example B—Not Scalable* Response Categories						
	1	2	3	4	5	6	7		1	2	3	4	5	6	7
English	X	X	X	X	X	X	X	English	X		X	X			X
Swedes		X	X	X	X	X	X	Swedes		X	X	X	X		
Poles			X	X	X	X	X	Poles	X		X		X		X
Mexicans				X	X	X	X	Mexicans	X	X	X				
Koreans					X	X	X	Koreans		X	X				X

[18] Emory S. Bogardus, *Immigration and Race Attitudes* (Boston: Heath, 1929).

[19] Emory S. Bogardus, *Social Distance* (Yellow Springs, Ohio: Antioch Press, 1959).

[20] We have reversed the position of the row headings and column headings from that in the questionnaire in order to make the measures run horizontally. In effect the social distince of the respondent from each nationality is indicated by the distance to the point where the first X is placed.

Figure 8. *Bogardus Social-Distance Scale*

Please read the following description of different degrees of personal "closeness" which people might be willing to permit in their relations with members of particular groups.

1. Would admit to close kinship by marriage.
2. Would admit to my club as personal chums.
3. Would admit to my street as a neighbor.
4. Would admit to my occupation in my country.
5. Would admit to citizenship in my country.
6. Would admit as visitors only to my country.
7. Would exclude from my country.

Now consider the groups of people listed below. Place an "X" under the number which most nearly represents the degree of closeness (as described above) to which you would be willing to admit members of each group. Give your reaction to each group as a whole. Do not give your reaction to the best or the worst members that you have known.

GROUP	1	2	3	4	5	6	7
Armenians							
Bulgarians							
Canadians							
Chinese							
Czechoslovaks							
Danes							
Dutch							
English							
French							
French-Canadians							
Finns							
Germans							
Greeks							
Hindus							
Hungarians							
Indians (American)							
Irish							
Italians							

Figure 8 continued

GROUP	1	2	3	4	5	6	7
Japanese							
Jew—German							
Jew—Russian							
Koreans							
Mexicans							
Mulattos							
Negroes							
Norwegians							
Portuguese							
Filipinos							
Poles							
Roumanians							
Russians							
Serbo-Croatians							
Scotch							
Scotch-Irish							
Spanish							
Syrians							
Swedish							
Turks							
Welsh							

The patterns in Example A all show that the seven response categories are scalable, because if the respondent checks response 1, "admit to close kinship by marriage," then he checked every category to the right of that. This regularity of pattern holds for all five of the ethnic groups in Example A. In Example B we see an entirely different picture. The X's are almost randomly distributed and make no social-psychological sense as we try to empathize with the respondent. For example, why should he be willing to have an Englishman marry his daughter but unwilling to have him as a fellow club member or even as a visitor to the United States? Similarly, none of the other four response patterns makes sense. For this reason there must be some objective and valid way of determining whether any set of items actually belongs on the same scale (unidimensionality) and what ordinal position the items occupy on that dimension. Such procedures should be applicable to all cases whether or not the responses are dichotomous. These empirical procedures were developed by Thurstone, Likert, and Guttman.

The Bogardus scale, unlike those designed by Thurstone, Likert, and Guttman, was not used to rank individuals on a scale according to the amount of a certain attitude they had. Instead, it was used to rank the different ethnic and racial groups on a scale according to their relative social distance from a sample of respondents. The Social Distance Scale was scored by calculating the mean value of the responses given by the sample of respondents toward each of the racial or ethnic groups. Thus, a mean value was assigned to each of the groups, but no score was given to each respondent. There is no reason why the same data could not be used to assign an attitude score to each respondent. Instead of social distance we would have to use some concept such as "ethnocentrism" or "exclusiveness" to apply to the total numerical value of the person's responses to all of the ethnic groups.

The Bogardus Social Distance Scale is still widely used in forms adapted for the particular problem at hand.

Thurstone's Attitude Scales

While Bogardus, a sociologist at the University of Southern California, was concentrating on the study of racial and ethnic groups in relation to immigration and social distance, Thurstone, a psychologist at the University of Chicago, was concentrating on finding methods of developing valid and reliable scales. He was concerned mainly with how to select the statements or questions for an attitude scale and how to assign scale values to the items.

Instead of depending, as Bogardus had done, upon his own empathy alone to order items for measuring people's attitudes, Thurstone obtained statements from many sources; he then submitted them to a group of "judges," who were asked to sort the statements (130 of them, in the case of the scale on attitudes toward the church) into eleven piles, with the first pile representing the most positive and the last the most negative statement about the church. Thus, the panel of judges determined the position of each item on the scale. After all the judges had given a scale value from 1 to 11 to each of the 130 items, Thurstone selected from the 130 a much smaller number for the final scale to be used with the larger population sample.

From all the judges' sortings, the median scale value and the inter-quartile range of the distribution were calculated for each item. Then three criteria were applied for the selection of items: (1) Items which had median values distributed along the *full range* of the scale were retained. (2) When two items had the same median scale value, the one with smallest *interquartile range* (which shows a high degree of agreement among the judges regarding the appropriate position of the item on the scale) was selected. (3) If there were enough items with small interquartile ranges, then items would be chosen to fall at as many *equal-appearing* intervals along the scale as possible. For example, in Figure 9 the following median scale values might be selected from all items having an interquartile range of less than 1.0 on the scale.

It is almost impossible to have actual median values which fall exactly on the ideal equal-appearing interval values on the scale. This

Figure 9. *Scale Values: Ideal and Actual*

Ideal	Actual
1.00	1.22
1.50	1.61
2.00	2.13
2.50	2.49
3.00	3.01
3.50	3.46
4.00	3.95
4.50	4.53
5.00	5.21
5.50	5.59
6.00	5.99
6.50	6.52
7.00	7.19
7.50	7.53
8.00	8.01
8.50	8.53
9.00	9.02
9.50	9.60
10.00	10.30
10.50	10.53
11.00	10.78

is especially improbable when the additional criterion of a small interquartile range has to be simultaneously applied.

Thurstone attempted to devise an interval scale with equal units. But his intellectual honesty forced him to call the units on his scales "equal-appearing" intervals in recognition of the fact that these units appeared to the judges, on the average, to be equal. The equal-appearing interval method was based upon the time-honored psychophysical concept of the JND, or "just-noticeable-difference," in which the difference between the physical weights of two objects must reach a certain magnitude before a person can reliably tell which is heavier by lifting each in turn or at the same time in different hands. As the weights of the objects increase, the absolute difference in weight must be greater before a person can detect a difference. Thus, the reasoning is that two weights or two attitude statements are not different psychologically unless they can be reliably judged so by the human mind. The direct application of this principle to attitude measurement would require that the panel of judges make "paired comparisons" between all possible pairs of statements. Thus, if we begin with 130 items, each judge would be required to make 8,385 judgments; if 100 judges were used, 838,500 judgments would have to be made. It is understandable that Thurstone sought a more efficient and practical way to arrive at a scale!

Even if there were a practical way to make over 8,000 paired comparisons, it is highly doubtful that it would be worthwhile to do so, since there are two basic differences between using the method to determine the threshold of weight discrimination in humans and using it to determine the threshold of discrimination among attitude statements. First, in dealing with weight discrimination, there is an independent measure of weight (the balance scales), which directly measures weight without relying on human sensory discrimination. This allows the "just-noticeable-difference" to be expressed in units on the ratio scale of physical weight. Unfortunately, there is no independent measure in the case of attitude measurement.

Second, the psychophysical problem of weight discrimination does not involve establishing the unidimensionality of the scale. There is no danger that the balance scales will be influenced by the shape, color, temperature, or hardness of the object, so there is no problem of introducing additional dimensions to confuse the measurement. In the case of judgments of differences in weight, there is some danger that these other factors might cause confusion if they were not controlled by selecting objects of the same shape, color, temperature, and hardness, but this controlled selection is easily done.

According to the Thurstone method, the researcher who initially selects the items simply assumes that his own empathy is sufficient to select items relevant to one and only one dimension. He does not ask the judges which items belong on the specified dimension but asks only where on the continuum each item belongs. Furthermore, he does not ask the ultimate respondents to the scale whether they perceive the items as being relevant to the single continuum, nor does he ask them where on the continuum each item belongs.[21]

So, while borrowing the concept of the JDN from psychophysics to use in social psychology, Thurstone also borrowed the assumption that unidimensionality could be taken for granted and that we could focus on the problem of discovering more precisely where each item belongs on the dimension. This was an extremely serious flaw in the Thurstone method, since much evidence can be marshalled to show that what one person assumes to belong on a scale another person would reject.

All of these shortcomings are dealt with by both the Likert and the Guttman scaling methods. Likert solved some of the problems of the Thurstone method, except for finding a valid procedure for establishing unidimensionality, and established simpler procedures. Later Guttman concentrated his attack upon the central problem of testing and measuring the amount of unidimensionality of a set of items. Let us look first at the Likert method.

The Likert Scaling Method

The Likert method overcomes two shortcomings which Thurstone recognized in his equal-appearing intervals approach. Instead of using a panel of judges to select the items from among those collected by the researcher, Likert used the actual respondents whose attitude was being measured. This method[22] circumvented the untested assumption made by Thurstone that the judges thought the same way about the statements as the subjects whose attitudes were to be measured.

Another difference in the Likert method is that, instead of having the respondent simply select from among the statements those with which he agreed, he was to respond to *all items* on a five-point scale of intensity, which in the most abstract form was as follows:

---

[21] For details of the Thurstone method of scaling consult the original work, L. L. Thurstone and E. J. Chave, *The Measurement of Attitudes* (Chicago: University of Chicago Press, 1929); or a simplified exposition like William J. Goode and Paul K. Hatt, *Methods in Social Research* (New York: McGraw-Hill Book Co., 1952), pp. 261-72.

[22] Gardner Murphy and Rensis Likert, *Public Opinion and the Individual* (New York: Harper, 1938).

__Strongly Agree __Agree __Uncertain __Disagree __Strongly Disagree

After the subjects had responded to the whole list of statements, the method of *internal consistency* was used to select the items belonging on the one relevant dimension. This was done by correlating the value of the response to one question with the mean value of all the items for that person. This process is repeated for all items in the original set; then those items which have a low correlation are eliminated from the scale. After these items are eliminated, all the tests must be rescored, using only those items which correlate highly with the total score on the test.

The value of the Likert method was mainly in its use of the respondents themselves as the basis of item selection and in the use of the intensity-scaled response to each item. The former made the scale more valid for the ultimate respondents, and the latter made it possible to have a wider range of scores with fewer items. For example, the possible range of scores for a ten-item attitude scale would be 0 to 10 for Thurstone's method and 10 to 50 (or 0 to 40) for the Likert method.

It seems that the Likert method is at least as valid as the Thurstone method and is much less laborious because it eliminates the use of judges and reduces the total number of items needed without increasing the amount of labor in the item-selection process.

The serious weakness in the Likert method is shared with the Thurstone method of equal-appearing intervals, which does not clearly establish that the items actually belong on a unidimensional continuum. While the Thurstone method relies mainly on the insight of the researcher who selects the set of items to be submitted to the judges, the Likert method tries to apply a more objective method of testing the internal consistency of the set of items by correlating the values of the responses to a particular item to the total score. In our judgment, this method of testing internal consistency shares the basic weakness of all methods of "item analysis," which is succinctly stated by Guttman as follows:[23]

> Item analysis does not attempt to see how well items can be reproduced from the total score, but rather it attempts to do *just the opposite*; item analysis investigates how well the total score can be estimated from each item *separately*.

Therefore, if the objective is to construct a scale so that any two per-

[23] Samuel A. Stouffer *et al.*, *Measurement and Prediction*, Vol. 4 in *Studies in Social Psychology in World War II* (Princeton: Princeton University Press, 1950), p. 184.

sons with the same score are known (within a certain amount of error of reproducibility) to have the same *pattern* of responses to all items on the scale, it is clear that this is not accomplished when we select the items by various techniques of item analysis.

It can be demonstrated that under certain circumstances an item which does correlate highly with the total score does not belong on the same dimension with the other items in the set used to obtain that total score. Furthermore, items which do not correlate with the total score may actually belong on the continuum. To quote Guttman again:

> For example, consider a dichotomous question . . . in which 60% of the people said "Yes" and 40% said "No," and where "Yes" is more favorable than "No." . . . If a person said "Yes" to the question, we *cannot* know his rank (in the total scores) very closely from this information alone; it can be anything from the 40th to the 100th percentile. If he said "No" his rank could be anything between zero and the fortieth percentile.[24]

Thus, the internal consistency method treats each item as a separate predictor of the total score. These separate predictors need not necessarily belong to the same unidimensional scale; they may belong to several intercorrelating scales, or each may constitute a one-item scale with a five-point response.

It remained for Guttman to attack directly the most basic problem of validity by establishing a method for determining whether or not a particular set of items in fact belongs to a single dimension.

ATTITUDE SCALES AND THE SEMANTIC DIFFERENTIAL

To this point we have been stressing the differences among the approaches of Bogardus, Thurstone, Likert, and Guttman to scaling attitudes. Before presenting a detailed treatment of the Guttman technique, which provides the most effective test of the unidimensionality of any set of attitude-questionnaire items, it would be helpful to show the common assumptions underlying these four methods. To do this we will briefly contrast them with Osgood's Semantic Differential technique.

Osgood[25] searched for ways of measuring the connotative meaning of words to show how the subtle feelings conveyed by a word could

---

[24] *Ibid.*

[25] Charles E. Osgood; George J. Suci; and Percy H. Tannenbaum, *The Measurement of Meaning* (Urbana, Illi.: University of Illinois Press, 1957).

vary from culture to culture even when the denotative dictionary definitions are identical. He found three most salient dimensions of the connotative emanations of a word, which he calls *evaluation*, *activity* and *potency*. It is the *evaluation* dimension that most closely fits the notion of attitude as measured by Bogardus, Thurstone, Likert, and Guttman.

Osgood's evaluative connotation of a word is actually people's attitude toward the object represented by that word. Osgood, however, made an assumption that distinguishes his method from the others dealt with here. He assumed that pairs of polar adjectives (such as *fair-unfair*, *clean-dirty*, *valuable-worthless*, *hard-soft*) can be found which can validly be applied to evaluate the feeling tone associated with many different words or concepts. Thus, the same set of response items could be used to measure attitude toward different social objects or words. This is in direct contrast to the other methods, which assume that a different set of items must be tailor-made to reflect faithfully one's attitude toward different objects. The Bogardus method leans slightly in this direction by assuming that the same set of statements could be used to reflect degrees of social distance of the respondent from a long list of nationalities, religions, or races of people. But for Bogardus all the social objects were in one category, called ethnic groups, so the objects were more homogenous than a set as divergent as capital punishment, communism, democracy or Swede. At this point we will not elaborate the relative merits or feasibility of specific versus generalized attitude scales. A good discussion of the generalized attitude scale appears in Osgood,[26] and a specific example of some of the strengths and limitations of the generalizability of specific polar pairs of adjectives to different attitude objects can be found in an experiment by Brinton.[27]

Certainly, it would be highly efficient if we could find a set of pairs of polar adjectives which could be used to measure attitudes toward any object and to have the assurance that these polar pairs would be valid for all time, for all respondents in all cultures. Even though there is considerable evidence that this is impossible, the opposite proposition, that a new set of attitude items must always be devised for each attitude object, for each different culture, for each sample of respondents, and for each historical period, is not necessarily correct. Instead of waiting for a resolution of this controversy, we can be content with learning how to determine whether or not a particular set of items, in a particular case, constitutes a valid and reliable unidimensional scale.

[26] *Ibid.*, p. 195f.
[27] James E. Brinton, "Deriving an Attitude Scale from Semantic Differential Data," *Public Opinion Quarterly* 25 (1961): 289-95.

A second basic difference between the Semantic Differential technique and unidimensional attitude scales, as they have been developed and applied, is signalled in the word *semantic*. Since semantics deals with the relationship between the *symbol* (word) and the *referent* (object or idea for which the word stands), the Semantic Differential technique usually takes the isolated word as its unit of analysis. The person is asked to respond to a single word or a series of unrelated words. In contrast, the attitude scale requires the person to respond to a statement which may vary from a short phrase to a paragraph or more. The first technique assumes that a word has a layer of connotative meaning that is not basically influenced by its verbal context.

A third difference is that the Semantic Differential method emphasizes the difference in the connotative meaning of a word from one group of people to another, while the unidimensional scale emphasizes the difference in attitude strength from one individual to another. Thus, the end product of the Semantic Differential is a value assigned to a *word*, while the end product of the unidimensional attitude scale is a value assigned to a *person*. In the former case we are placing the connotative meaning of a word on a scale, and in the latter we are locating an individual's attitude strength on a scale.

A fourth difference is that the Semantic Differential may use each of the dimensions bounded by a pair of polar adjectives (good-bad, fair-unfair, safe-dangerous, etc.) as *separate* dimensions, so that each single item may be considered as a scale in itself, while in the unidimensional scale it must be shown that all the items in the questionnaire belong on a *single* dimension. In the former method the data may be presented as a multifaceted profile of the connotative meaning of a word, while the latter method results in a quantitative distribution of an individual's scores.

With the perspective gained by this distinction between unidimensional scales designed for the measurement of individuals' attitudes and multivariable evaluative profiles, let us return to our original pursuit of the unidimensional scale and explore the Guttman unidimensional scaling method in detail. In Chapter 2, *Building a Guttman Scale*, we will first explain the meaning of unidimensionality, which is the essence of Guttman scaling. We will then show how to go about discovering and selecting items which have a good chance of belonging on the same psychological dimension. Finally, we will show how to refine the *metric* (measuring sensitivity), of the items in the scale.

Chapter 2.   Building a Guttman Scale

THE ESSENCE OF GUTTMAN SCALING: UNIDIMENSIONALITY

In Chapter 1 we showed that the most fundamental property common to all types of scale, even the nominal scale, is *dimensionality*. Then, in reviewing the scaling methods developed by Bogardus, Thurstone, and Likert, we showed that the most fundamental weakness of all three was their failure to develop an adequate empirical test of the unidimensionality of the set of items as applied to the people whose attitudes were being measured.

Bogardus assumed that unidimensionality was self-evident in the content of the items which were considered to be markers of social distance. Thurstone assumed that unidimensionality was established through the insight of the person selecting the items, so that the panel of judges could concentrate on the quantitative location of each item on the assumed unidimensional continuum. Likert tried to develop an objective, empirical method of establishing unidimensionality through the internal consistency test of correlation. None of these approaches is adequate for the basic task of scaling. It is precisely this problem of testing a set of items for unidimensionality which is the central focus of Guttman scaling theory and techniques.

Guttman[1] has clearly demonstrated the fallacy in assuming that the group of judges can validly arrange a set of statements into a rank order on a continuum. He demonstrated that in making an *a priori* rank ordering of qualitative response categories the assumption of rank position often does not hold up under empirical test. For ex-

---

[1] Samuel A. Stouffer *et al.*, *Measurement and Prediction*, Vol. 4 in *Studies in Social Psychology in World War II* (Princeton: Princeton University Press, 1950), pp. 187-8.

ample, the following question was assumed to have four responses representing four degrees of favorableness of attitude toward Russia.

"With which *one* of these statements concerning postwar relations with Russia do you come closest to agreeing?"

(1) It is very important to keep on friendly terms with Russia, and we should make every possible effort to do so.

(2) It is important for the U.S. to be on friendly terms with Russia, but not so important that we should make too many concessions to her.

(3) If Russia wants to keep on friendly terms with us, we shouldn't discourage her, but there is no reason why we should make any special effort to be friendly.

(4) We shall be better off it we have just as little as possible to do with Russia.

To test the assumption that the four statements actually indicated the degrees of favorableness intended, the researchers asked the question of a sample of 3,000 enlisted men in the following form:

"Do you agree with this statement?"

(1) It is very important to keep on friendly terms with Russia, and we should make every possible effort to do so.
___ Agree
___ Disagree
___ Undecided

Similarly, each man was asked if he agreed or disagreed with each of the remaining three statements. A subsequent scalogram analysis showed that these four questions did not form a scale. For example, some of those who agreed with statement 4 also agreed with statement 1.

MEASURING UNIDIMENSIONALITY

The central purpose of the Guttman scaling method is to test unidimensionality, and the basic measure of unidimensionality is the *coefficient of reproducibility*. By reproducibility Guttman meant that the relations between the responses to any set of scalable items must be such that one and only one pattern of responses to the whole set of items corresponds to a particular total score obtainable by any respondent. To illustrate this concept, consider a series of examples proceeding from the simple and obvious to the more complex and less obvious.

The condition of reproducibility holds when the scale used to arrive at the score is *cumulative*—that is to say, when the items can be put in such an order that everyone who said "yes" to question 2 also said "yes" to question 1, and everyone who said "yes" to question 6 also said "yes" to questions 1, 2, 3, 4, and 5. Immediately, this suggests that the Guttman rationale is more closely related to the Bogardus Social-Distance scale than to the Thurstone or Likert scale. In the Bogardus scale the cumulative nature seemed so obvious that he did not devise a technique to verify it quantitatively.

In the physical world we know that if an object is three feet long it is longer than one foot and longer than two feet. If we melt a pot of ice cubes and raise the temperature to the boiling point, we know that the temperature had to pass through $33°$, $40°$, $50°$, $100°$, $150°$, and $200°$ to get to $212°$. In the psychological world we know that a person who is capable of solving multiplication problems is also capable of adding, that a person capable of doing long division is also capable of doing multiplication, and that a person who can do square roots can also do long division. Thus, if we know he can do square roots, we know that he can add, multiply, and divide. In other words, learning certain types of mathematics is a cumulative, one-way process, and the different types of problems represent a hierarchy of difficulty or complexity.

In the social world we know that a black American who would not mind if his sister married a German-Jewish-American also would not mind if a German-Jewish-American lived in his neighborhood. This is the basic idea of the cumulative, and therefore unidimensional, scale relationship between items which mark ordinal points on a continuum.

In his scaling method Guttman provides an objective procedure for testing and measuring the amount of unidimensionality in a set of attitude statements rather than assuming or intuiting the unidimensionality, as his predecessors did. However, Guttman emphasizes the method of measuring the unidimensionality of a set of items *after* they are administered to a sample of respondents and does not deal thoroughly with the question of how items can be selected to increase the probability that they will prove unidimensional.

But selection is an important process. For this reason we will give some suggestions and procedures for obtaining a set of items before describing the technique of testing the set for unidimensionality. Discovering, selecting, and constructing items for the scale is a creative process which cannot be reduced to a mechanical procedure;

there are conceptual frameworks to be used as guidelines to increase the probability of success.

DISCOVERING AND SELECTING SCALE ITEMS

Attitude scale items do not drop upon us like manna; nor can we depend upon armchair intuition to supply a set of items that will prove to be scalable. A set of attitude items must be discovered, selected, constructed, revised, and tested. There is no guarantee in advance that a set of items can be found which will define any single dimension or attitude that the researcher imagines to exist. Before it is possible to discover, select, and construct items that will prove to be unidimensional certain conditions must be met, and in sequential order. If the first condition is not present in empirical reality, there is no value in attempting to meet the second. Similarly, if the second condition has not been met, there is no value in attempting the third.

(1) There must actually be an attitude toward the object (class of objects, event, or idea) in the minds of the people in the population to be sampled and tested.

(2) A set of statements about the object must be found which have meaning to the members of the sample and which elicit from them a response that is a valid indicator of that attitude.

(3) The items in this set of statements or questions must represent different degrees along a single dimension.

We must not assume, merely because the researcher has an attitude toward something or believes that others do, that the population to be tested actually has such an attitude at the moment. We cannot even assume that the object of attitude in a certain population at one time is also the object of attitude at another time. In one society or subculture there may be a strong attitude toward Jews, poverty, the mentally ill, the President of the United States, or the United Nations; in another society or subculture these same objects may evoke no feeling either positive or negative. People at different stages of the life cycle have different objects of attitude. To one generation such symbols as Nazi, Pearl Harbor, the Depression, or Tommy Dorsey are objects of feeling, while to another generation they evoke no feeling.

Less obviously, even when a general category such as "black" remains the object of strong attitudes over a period of time, the nature of the attitude may change considerably. At one time the issue might be whether blacks should be free or slave, at another whether they should be allowed to vote. Later the issue might be whether or not they should be allowed to use the same public restaurants, swimming pools, theaters, barber shops, and churches as whites. At another time the main issue might center about the political or economic sphere of activities. Therefore items must be selected which place the object of the attitude in a social context relevant to the times.

We must first discover whether the hypothetical attitude actually exists at the present time in the population to be tested. If such an attitude does exist, then we must discover, select, and construct items currently relevant to the attitude. The general object, the more specific issue, and the particular vocabulary used must be such that they correspond to the cultural reality and strike a responsive chord in the subjective orientations (attitudes, beliefs, and knowledge) of the respondent.

Discovering Unidimensional Items[2]

To some extent attitude scale items are discovered by methods ranging from pure serendipity to more systematic application of sympathetic introspection, participant observation, unstructured interviewing, and reading. In Guttman's terminology, we must explore the "universe of content" for the attitude being studied.

Sympathetic Introspection. The discovery process for Bogardus, Thurstone, and Likert included sympathetic introspection by the researcher and others who were asked to furnish statements and questions to elicit an attitudinal response from some groups of respondents. The success of this sympathetic introspection process by the researcher and those he asks for help requires that they all belong to the same culture or subculture as the persons to whom the attitude scale is ultimately to be administered.

Participant Observation. By direct participant observation the researcher can simply listen to spontaneous conversations around him concerning the object of the attitude in which he is interested. Even though people's attitudes might rarely surface in the form of verbal statements, these rare occasions furnish insight into which aspects of the object, event, or issue are emotionally charged. One indicator of

[2] If you have the rare circumstance in which Semantic Differential responses on many pairs of polar adjectives have been given in relationship to the attitude object in which you are interested, it is possible to select a few pairs to constitute a unidimensional scale according to Guttman criteria. One account of this procedure is given in James E. Brinton, "Deriving an Attitude Scale from Semantic Differential Data," *Public Opinion Quarterly* 25 (1961): 289-95.

the existence of a strong attitude is the tendency for people to polarize into pro and anti groups.

If the researcher is totally unfamiliar with the social setting of the attitude in question, he should try the participant-observation method before he intervenes in the social process by interviewing. At first it might be fruitful to introduce some informal interviewing[3] into the participant-observation process in order to obtain further insights into and clues to questions to be used and areas to be probed in the formal interviewing.

Interviewing. Formal interviewing may also be very fruitful and can be done more directly and efficiently than participant observation. However, the word "formal" in this context does not mean highly structured. The interviewing must be geared to discovery rather than measurement.[4] This discovery process should not begin with a fixed sequence of questions or any questions with answer categories already supplied or implied by the wording of the question. Instead, it should begin with a frank statement that the interviewer is trying to discover how people express either positive or negative attitudes toward the object in question. In order to avoid the ego-threat barrier, the interviewer may begin his questioning indirectly, by asking what the respondent thinks about what "others" who are pro and con think (say or feel) about the object of the attitude. For example:

"As you know, there is some talk now about whether to legalize marijuana, and some people are for it and others against."

(1) "Have you heard any discussion or read anything about this issue?"
(2) "What are some of the things you have heard or read about this issue?"
(3) "What are some of the arguments people might have for or against?"
(4) "Why are some people for it? Why are some against it?"
(5) "What sort of thing would a person opposed say?"
(6) "What sort of thing would a person in favor say?"

---

[3] By *informal interview* we mean informal conversation within the constraints of whatever role the participant observer has in the situation which is not the role of interviewer. The researcher in the informal interview has a systematic purpose in his conversations but does not take notes on the spot, does not promise anonymity to the respondent, and does not define the situation as an interview for the respondent. The interviewing aspect of the conversation in no way alters the nature of the informal conversation, but only alters the way in which the researcher thinks about what is said and systematically selects certain information as significant to his problem.

[4] Raymond L. Gorden, *Interviewing: Strategy, Techniques and Tactics* (Homewood, Ill.: Dorsey Press, 1975), pp. 66-74.

(7) "Who is against legalizing marijuana?"

(8) "Who is for legalizing marijuana?"

General questions such as these should unearth some emotion-laden statements to be used as stated or to be probed for raw material to use in constructing attitude statements.

The researcher should strive to discover the whole range of expression and should therefore include interviews with people taking extreme opposite positions.

Reading. If the object, issue, or event toward which the attitudes are manifested has been written about recently in newspapers, magazines, journals, or books, the researcher should seek the most polemical of these writings on both sides of the issue. These should provide raw materials for the construction of attitude items as well as background for participant observation and interviewing.

The discovery phase should reveal the emotionally charged issues, themes, or aspects of the object in question, the vocabulary used, some of the rationalizations given to support the views, and some of the general contexts of interpretation used by those who are pro and those who are con. This phase may produce a wealth of possible statements, but it will neither select the few most appropriate nor will it give the best semantic construction of the statements to be used. This is done in the selection and construction processes.

Selecting Unidimensional Items

Whatever method is used to collect the raw materials from the universe of content, the researcher is faced with the need to select from among the whole sample a smaller number of items which will act as a scale. Bogardus did this intuitively; Thurstone selected those which had equal-appearing intervals according to the median value assigned by a panel of judges.

Within the framework of the Guttman method, a preliminary selection of items must be made before they are administered to the respondents. Further selection can be done after the responses are obtained. We are concerned with the preliminary selection. It should be kept in mind throughout this discussion that any set of items comprising an attitude scale is only one sample of items from the larger *universe of content* involving a particular attitude. Thus, two researchers could arrive at different or overlapping sets of items, each of which could make up a perfect scale.

Although I have not found any systematic account by Guttman of how items are selected, I will present some of the basic criteria gleaned from other writers and from my own experiences in constructing scales.

Work with Only One Attitude.   There are several ways in which items can cause confusion by mixing more than one attitude. First, the wording of an item may not make it clear whether it refers to the respondent's attitude at some time in the past or in the present. Items should nearly always be worded so as to elicit the respondent's current attitude, which is usually more relevant and easier to report.

A second way of mixing attitudes in an item is to use a "double-barreled" statement. Often the raw, spontaneous attitudinal statement contains two statements in one, a situation that poses no contradiction to the person making the statement. Another person, however, might agree with one part of the statement and disagree with the other part. For example:

"Marijuana should be legalized and have no restrictions on being advertised."

Even though this statement might precisely express the position of one person encountered in exploratory field work, there is obviously no reason to expect everyone to accept this "package deal" of legalizing and advertising. A person might be opposed to both aspects of the statement, to the first aspect, the second aspect, or neither. The solution is simply to break the question into two:

"Marijuana should be legalized."

"There should be no legal restrictions on advertising marijuana."

A third way of building a mixture of attitudes into the same statement, even if it is not double-barrelled, is to use broad, ambiguous terminology with contains two or more objects toward which some people have different attitudes. For example:

"No one should use illegal drugs!"

This statement might be a legitimate scale item for one population, such as rural residents over 65 years of age, but it might present a real dilemma to populations who make a great distinction between marijuana, heroin, and LSD. Such groups might feel strongly that marijuana should be legalized but that use of the hard drugs should carry a stiff penalty.

It is in the initial exploratory field work that such distinctions must be discovered in the population where the attitude is to be measured. In the example used above, certain questions must be answered in the field work and applied in selecting the items. For instance: is there an attitude toward illegal drugs as a general category, or toward the use of a particular drug? Is the underlying criterion by which actions toward drugs are judged the legality of the drug, its effects on an individual, or its long-range effects upon society and community?

If we do not know the answers to such questions, we are in danger of devising a logically neat set of items that are unrelated to social reality as reflected in the universe of content.

Beware the Cognitive.[5] In general items should be selected in which the cognitive element is not predominant. Even though attitude theory and empirical studies show that a strong attitude does bias one's perception, memory, assumptions, and reasoning about the facts, it is still possible to make the cognitive element so overpowering in an item that only in the most extreme cases of either pro or anti attitude would the item elicit an attitudinal or affective response. For example, the following four statements represent four different mixtures of the affective and the cognitive:

(1) "Jews should not be allowed in medical schools."
(2) "There are already too many Jews in medical schools."
(3) "There are twice as many Jews as non-Jews in medical schools."
(4) "Over 59% of the students in medical schools are Jewish."

Statement (1) is purely affective and normative, dealing with what "should" be rather than with what is. Statement (2) introduces a flavor of the cognitive in the phrase "too many." Note that "too many" is not defined; the respondent may feel that anywhere from 1% to 50% is "too many." So the implied quantification of facts does not hamper his expression of feeling.

In statement (3) the cognitive intrudes very forcefully in the phrase "twice as many," which does not pretend to great exactness but does exclude the normative judgment implied in the phrase "too many." It is true that a person with strong prejudices and fears might be willing to accept this statement without worrying about the evidence since it would furnish proof of his contention that "if you let a few of them in they take over."

Statement (4) does not imply any normative judgment and reinforces the factual orientation by making the stated proportion of Jewish medical students more precise. This encourages the respondent to think in quantitative terms. If he does not have information on the situation, he will therefore take the neutral position of "don't know," "not sure," or "undecided," which would have nothing to do with his attitude. Also, if another respondent happened to have read

---

[5] Here we use the word "cognitive" to include various aspects of knowing such as perception, judgment, reasoning, remembering, and thinking, in contrast to the "affective" aspects of experience, such as feeling, desire, sentiment, or attitude.

the latest figures on enrollments in medical schools, he would know that the percentage of Jewish students was much lower than the 59% suggested. He could choose the answer "strongly disagree," whether he feels that 1% would be too many or that 59% would not be enough. Thus, forms (3) and (4) are relatively useless for eliciting attitudinal responses; forms (1) and (2) would be more effective.

Avoid Unique Experiences.   Even though we want to cover a variety of emotionally laden aspects of the object of the attitude, we must avoid selecting statements which represent rare orientations. For example, the following statement might be made by a Christian Scientist in discussing the drug issue:

> "God does not approve of our taking hard drugs or any other form of drug to try to force the body to do by chemical means what can only be done by faith in Him."

This statement may be strongly felt by the Christian Scientist but might pose a dilemma to the 98% of the sample who do not share his religious commitment, with the position it implies. The item would serve the function of selecting out Christian Scientists rather than discovering attitudes toward drug abuse.

Similarly, if we were trying to devise items to measure students' attitudes toward the Vietnam War, the following item would select out the people opposed to wars on principle rather than those opposing the Vietnam War specifically:

> "I am against participation in the Vietnam War or any other form of conflict in which one person takes the life of another."

When deciding which items to select for the scale from the available pool of statements we should look for the major themes and omit the minor ones. Then, within each of these major themes, look for statements that represent the full range of feelings.

Cover the Full Range of Attitudes.   Items should be selected which range all the way from the strongest pro to the strongest anti feelings. We need some positive statements with which all of the respondents will agree and other positive statements with which none will agree; we need some negative statements with which all respondents will agree and other negative statements with which none will agree. Unless we have such statements, we have no assurance that our scale is long enough to measure everyone's attitude. Because of his own attitude on the topic, the researcher may fail to include the full range, particularly at the end of the scale opposite to his view, because such statements may appear ridiculous to him.

It is true that we should try to select items representing the full range of the scale and that Guttman scaling analysis will tell us whether or not we have succeeded. But it is another matter to know how to judge the relative scale position of items in advance. Nevertheless, we must be able to do this at least crudely if we are to construct a valid scale.

We will continue the discussion of this problem of covering the full range in the next section, on the construction of items, with the understanding that it also applies to the selection of items. If we know how to construct the ideal *forms* of items, regardless of content, we are in a better position to recognize appropriately constructed items when we see them in the selection process. In practice, selection and construction often take place simultaneously to produce the type of items needed.

Laboratory Problem 1 gives you an opportunity to apply some of the principles of item selection by eliminating inappropriate items from those proposed for an attitude scale. (If you plan to hand in your solution to this and other Laboratory Problems you may want to reproduce the answer sheet from Appendix A, page 156.)

LABORATORY PROBLEM 1
Eliminating Irrelevant Items

Below are twenty statements proposed by students trying to construct a scale to measure current attitudes toward the Socialist Workers' Party (SWP) in a national sample of college students. Indicate which *seven* of these statements would probably be the *most inappropriate* (in their present form) for constructing a unidimensional attitude scale. Use the following key to indicate the main reason for rejecting each of these seven items.

Key

1-Too broad or vague
2-Confuses past and present attitudes
3-More than one attitude is involved
4-Too cognitive, not affective enough
5-Experience too idiosyncratic to apply to many respondents

____ (1) "The SWP is the best political organization on the American scene."
____ (2) "The SWP is the fastest growing party in the United States."
____ (3) "I strongly support the SWP and its activities."
____ (4) "When I see the behavior of the leaders at the SWP meeting it turns my stomach."
____ (5) "I feel that the SWP is probably doing some good."

___ (6) "The SWP has never done any harm and may do some good some day."

___ (7) "Radical political parties give me a pain in the neck."

___ (8) "The SWP is too unrealistic and autocratic to suit my taste."

___ (9) "I would like to get to know an SWP member so we could talk about politics."

___(10) "The SWP should be given a chance to be heard by everyone in the United States."

___(11) "In general I love radical political organizations."

___(12) "When I first heard about SWP it seemed like something resurrected from the past."

___(13) "The SWP should not be allowed to send their literature through the U.S. mails."

___(14) "The SWP should not be encouraged to grow in membership."

___(15) "The SWP does not aim at any relevant kind of social change."

___(16) "The SWP and the Black Muslims are very constructive politically."

___(17) "The leadership of the SWP is really hypocritical."

___(18) "My initial impression of the SWP was quite positive."

___(19) "The SWP should simply be outlawed."

___(20) "The SWP members should all be put in jail."

REFINING THE CALIBRATION OF THE ITEMS

In the previous sections we have been concerned with the discovery and selection of raw items. Now we will discuss methods of calibrating the items already selected. We shall be mainly concerned with two things: how to cover the full range of attitudes, and how to obtain many gradations along the continuum. We include both of these aspects in our definition of calibrating a set of questionnaire items.

Levels of Calibration Illustrated

To select or construct a set of items that will constitute a scale, we must have questions or statements (with corresponding responses) which represent different degrees of attitude and cover the full range of attitudes toward the object in question. In attitude scales calibration is ordinal rather than either interval or ratio. Calibration is built into the attitude scale at three levels:

(1) *Content* (theme or aspect of the object at issue)
(2) *Facet* (psycho-semantic form of the statement or question)
(3) *Response* (form of agreement with a statement or answer to a question)

These three levels are usually developed in this order in constructing sets of attitude items.

Let us illustrate the three levels of calibration by constructing some items related to the attitudes of whites toward blacks. The illustration will deal with the content, facet, and response levels in that order, all related to the same attitude. Then we will describe each level of calibration in greater detail.

In the following three items, the *content* represents three degrees of pro and anti attitudes of whites toward blacks.

Pro: "I like the saying 'black is beautiful.'"

Neutral: "Blacks and whites are equally human."

Anti: "Blacks cannot be trusted with money."

Here we have assumed that a person responding "strongly agree" to the first statement would have to be more pro-black than a person responding the same way to the second statement, and that the same response to the third statement would indicate an anti feeling. The weakest point might be in the assumption that strong agreement with the second statement indicates neutrality instead of a positive attitude, but this assumption can be tested in the actual use of the scale, as will be explained later. The fact that these three items have an ordinal relationship is wholly dependent upon the attitudinal value assigned in the minds of the respondents to the three different content themes.

By using facet theory, we can reword each statement in as many as five different ways, representing five different ordinal positions on a continuum. "Expanding" each of the three *content* statements into five *facets* allows us to introduce further gradations of attitude, increasing the number of measuring points on our scale.

Let us illustrate how this is done by expanding the negative theme into its five facet forms, as shown in Figure 10. The first column shows that there are two general content aspects of any attitude statement or question. The first aspect deals with the *nature* of the object (including its relations to objects other than the respondent himself or his in-group). The second aspect is the respondent's *inter-*

Content Aspects	Facets	Rank Order	Wording of the Statement
Nature of the Object	Societal stereotype	1	"Most people feel that blacks cannot be trusted with money."
	Personal beliefs	2	"I feel that blacks cannot be trusted with money."
Interaction with the Object	Moral imperative	3	"People should not trust blacks with money."
	Hypothetical action	4	"Personally, I would not trust blacks with money."
	Real action	5	"I have actually refused to trust blacks with money."

Figure 10. *Five Facet Versions of a Content Statement*

action with the object. These two aspects can be further broken down into five facets which correlate with five degrees of ego-involvement for the respondent. Several studies have demonstrated empirically that the rank orders shown in column 3 above actually occur in practice.[6]

Grouping the five facets into two general aspects calls attention to the fact that the content of some attitude statements lends itself to only two or three of the five facet forms. Other statements can easily be reworded to include both content aspects and therefore all five of the facet forms. There is no need to use all five facets of every statement or even to use as many as the content will permit. The important thing is to be aware that these five possible facets exist as one way of obtaining a more sensitive calibration than could be obtained by varying the content themes alone.

The third level of calibration is built into the form of the *response* itself. This refinement can be superimposed upon the previous two levels of calibration to obtain a measuring instrument with more established points on the continuum. The response choices may be

[6] Louis Guttman, "A Structural Theory for Intergroup Beliefs and Action," *American Sociological Review* 24, No. 3 (June, 1959): 318-28; A. E. Dell Orto, *A Guttman Facet Analysis of the Racial Attitudes of Rehabilitation Counselor Trainees*, Unpublished doctoral dissertation, Michigan State University, 1970; U. G. Foa, "A Facet Approach to the Prediction of Commonalities," *Behavioral Science* 8 (1963): 220-26.

constructed to allow from two to seven gradations of response. Both
the Bogardus scale and the Thurstone scale allowed the respondent
only the simple dichotomous choice between agreeing with a statement or not. Thus the value of the response to each statement was
either 0 or 1, or in some cases –1 or +1. In the Likert-type items the
responses were usually on a five-point scale, as in item (4) below. The
response pattern according to the Guttman system may allow for
two, three, four, or five gradations, and different items in the same
scale may have a different number of allowable responses.

Now let us illustrate the response level of calibration by adding
response patterns to facet forms 4 and 5 in Figure 10.

(4) "Personally, I would not trust blacks with money."

___(1) Strongly agree
___(2) Agree
___(3) Undecided
___(4) Disagree
___(5) Strongly disagree

(5) "I have actually refused to trust blacks with money."

___(1) Much more often than whites
___(2) More often than whites
___(3) About the same as whites
___(4) Less often than whites
___(5) Much less often than whites
___ X No opportunity

Note that the fifth facet form asks how the respondent has actually acted. Since not all whites are in circumstances where they have an
opportunity to trust or distrust blacks with money, we must add the
sixth choice, "no opportunity." (This is one of the weaknesses of the
fifth facet form. In the cases where the "no opportunity" category
applies, the item cannot be scored to contribute to either a pro- or
an anti-black attitude score.)

Example (4) above could be improved by using a question instead
of a statement and by making the answer choices *comparative with
whites*, as in the following example:

"How much would you personally trust blacks with money?"

___(1) Much less than whites
___(2) Less than whites
___(3) Same as whites
___(4) More than whites
___(5) Much more than whites

In this type of item it is important to provide a set of answers comparing the relative amount of trust of blacks versus whites; otherwise there is a danger of introducing an extraneous variable other than attitude which accounts for differences in responses from one respondent to another. This extraneous dimension is illustrated in the following faulty revision of item (5):

"How much money would you loan a black fellow-worker who asked for a loan and promised to repay in two weeks?"

——(1) Nothing
——(2) Up to $1.00
——(3) Up to $5.00
——(4) Up to $25.00
——(5) Up to $50.00

These answer categories appear to be more precise than those in the original item (5), but an extraneous variable has been introduced. We do not know whether a respondent who said he would loan "nothing" answered thusly because he had no money, because he would refuse to loan money to anyone regardless of color, or because he discriminates against blacks. The comparative item avoids this trap. (A more detailed treatment of the many possible forms of answers will be offered later. Here the point is merely to illustrate how the response calibration is added to the content theme and facet calibrations for further refinement of the scale.)[7]

We have just sketched the general process by which we can select and construct a set of items which have a high probability of falling at different points along the full range of the scale by (a) using positive and negative content items, (b) by expressing the same content in five facet forms, and (c) by using response forms which express varying degrees of attitude. This three-level process represents a progressive expansion of the possible number of scores produced by the scale, as is shown in Figure 11.

---

[7] It might seem prudent to construct items (4) and (5) above by omitting answer choices 1 and 5 in each case since we are not sure that respondents will generally be able to make a reliable distinction between answers 1 and 2 or between 4 and 5. However, there is nothing to lose by including them, and something may be gained because in the subsequent Guttman and analysis it is possible empirically to determine whether these distinctions are reliably made. If they are not reliable in the case of a particular question, we simply "collapse" the two categories into one, giving both types of responses the same value. This would give the same scores as if we had omitted the extreme answer categories initially. If the distinctions *are* reliably made, then we have a scale with a wider range of scores and greater sensitivity, and this will reduce the number of tie scores, which must be avoided if we are to use the scale scores in rank correlation with other variables in the study. Collapsing categories will be discussed in detail later.

Figure 11. *Levels of Calibration Multiplied To Give Range of Scores*

Levels	Calibration (Multiplied)	Possible Range of Scores
I. Content Theme	Three content items with dichotomous "agree" or "disagree" answers	0 to 3
II. Facet	Five facets of each of the three content theme items gives 15 items with dichotomous answers.	0 to 15
III. Response	Five facets of each content item with five-point answer ranges.	0 to 60*

*This range assumes that the five-point answer responses will be scored as ranging from 0 through 4. If they were scored as ranging from 1 through 5 the possible range would be 15 to 75 which is still a range of 60 points. If the response were scored as ranging from $-2, -1, 0, +1, +2$, then the range of total scores on the scale would be from -30 to $+30$.

This table was devised only to illustrate the three-level calibration. We do not suggest that in practice you should begin with only three content items and expand the number by constructing five facet forms of each. The attempt to squeeze the maximum range of 60 points out of so few content items would be undesirable in practice, for a number of reasons.

(1) The respondent might feel that the series of statements is highly contrived and tedious when so many questions sound very similar in content and vary only slightly in wording.

(2) In practice not all five of the facets always lend themselves to a particular content. As pointed out earlier, some content statements which deal with the *nature of the object* cannot be translated into facets (3), (4), or (5), which deal with the respondent's *relationship to that object*.

(3) As pointed out earlier, the fifth facet form is not appropriate to respondents who have little or no opportunity to interact with the object of the attitude.

(4) If the real universe of attitude items includes a wide variety of content themes, as many as possible should be represented in the sample of making up the scale so there is no need to begin with so few content items.

In the preceding pages we have tried to present an overview of how the three levels of calibration multiply the numerical range of the scale. We did not pause to describe each of the levels in detail. Now we will go back to the three levels to explain in greater depth the nature of the choices involved.

Content as Calibration

Of all the steps in the practical task of making up a Guttman uni-dimensional scale, the step that is the most neglected in the literature is the initial one: obtaining a set of items which have a good chance of being scalable. It is of little practical value to know how to apply the Guttman test of unidimensionality if each time we find that the set of items does not constitute a scale. Even though the set of items may be improved by eliminating some items or by collapsing answer categories, sets of items must be selected which are roughly scalable to begin with or there is no way of knowing which items are out of line.

All the content themes we have found fall into two broad general types. The first type comprises themes that describe the essential nature of the object of attitude, including its relationship to other objects of attitude. The second type are themes that describe the respondent's relationship to the object. We will refer to the first type as *essence* themes and the second type as *interaction* themes.

Essence Themes. An essence theme may be a statement of *criteria of judgment.* In a judgment of anything as good or bad there are usually some criteria, either directly given in support, vaguely implied, or silently assumed. In my experience there seem to be three criteria themes which generally fall into an ordinal scale if other variables are held constant in the wording. They can be represented on a continuum as follows:

-3	-2	-1	0	+1	+2	+3
Immoral	Illegal	Impractical		Practical	Legal	Moral
ANTI						*PRO*

Let us illustrate these six positions on the attitude continuum using themes expressing attitudes toward the Vietnam War:

(1) "The United States had no moral right to slaughter thousands of Vietnamese in a war that by the wildest stretch of the imagination could not be called defensive."

(2) "The so-called Vietnam War was illegal. The war had not been declared by the U.S. Congress, nor had it any legal sanction by the United Nations as a police action."

(3) "There was no way that the United States could win a mili-

tary victory in Vietnam, and any massive attempt to do so
might have triggered an all-out atomic war."

(4) "It was possible for the United States to win a military victory
in Vietnam to preserve an independent South Vietnam."

(5) "The U.S. armed forces did not need any formal legal man-
date for being in Vietnam from either the U.S. Congress or the
United Nations."

(6) "The United States simply could not shirk its moral responsi-
bility to protect the weak against Communist aggression in
Vietnam."

Although I have not done definitive research, I feel that morality
statements almost always represent a stronger position either pro or
anti than do legality or practicality statements. However, I am less
sure about the ordinal relationship between the legality and practicality statements. Their relative position on the scale is sometimes
complicated by the fact that many people feel there is a conflict
between morality and legality, in which case both morality and practicality may take precedence over legality.

Another essence theme may be called the *mutability* theme. Even
though we perceive an object as being bad (immoral, illegal, or im-
practical), some "bad" objects are considered correctible and others
evil beyond redemption. Things that are beyond redemption are
more evil than things that can be redeemed. This ordinal calibration
applies more obviously when the object of attitude is a person, a
class of persons, or a group of persons—for example, the President
of the United States, black radicals, or Congress. The six statements
below, for example, are intended to represent degrees of attitude toward the President of the United States, from more to less negative,
based on degrees of mutability.

(1) "No amount of political persuasion or reasoning from evidence could change the President's basic lack of concern for
the poor."

(2) "Only the most highly organized political pressure could ever
change the President's failure to act on behalf of the poor."

(3) "Systematic persuasion by grass-roots politicians over a period
of time could change the President's lack of concern for the
poor."

(4) "The President's apparent lack of concern for the poor could
be changed by presenting some dramatic evidence of the
amount of poverty in this country."

(5) "The President has thus far shown little public concern for the
poor only because of his preoccupation with other crises such
as the Vietnam War, the balance of international trade, and
inflation at home."

(6) "Although the President has to date shown little public concern for the poor, he is probably already planning basic reforms to help the poor, which will be instituted as soon as they are ready."

Even though there are other small differences in the wording of the six statements, the most consistent and salient difference is in the degree to which they express the belief that the basic sin of omission is correctable in this person's case. Note that even though the statements deal with relationships between the President and other objects and forces in the historical scene, none of the statements depicts any interactional relationship between the President and the respondent or his in-group. For this reason we include the mutability concept under the larger category of *essence* rather than under *relationships*, as defined above.

The calibration in the mutability theme is in the different degrees of redeemability in the nature of the object. Gradations of redeemability may be expressed in terms of the abstract probability of its being done, the types of force needed to do the job, or some more abstract or purely quantitative representation of the amount of energy that would have to be expended to affect redemption. The object may then be considered to be beyond redemption either because it is absolutely irredeemable or because it is not worth the cost of redemption.

A third essence theme is the *ends-means* relationship. The ends-means criterion *simultaneously* considers both the ends and the means by using a set of items representing different combinations of efficient and inefficient means with positive and negative ends that locate four different ordinal positions on a unidimensional continuum as shown below.

Ends–Means Continuum

ANTI			PRO
Efficient means to negative ends.	Inefficient means to negative ends.	Inefficient means to positive ends.	Efficient means to positive ends.

The means-ends theme is not adaptable to all objects of attitude. It seems to be more appropriate for attitudes toward historical events, social issues, policies, and plans rather than toward people. In some cases people are judged according to the effect of their actions on history. Then the events, issues, policies, or plans are intertwined with people, and the means-ends continuum is applicable.

Below are two sets of four statements, each representing different degrees of attitude based on the four different *ends-means* combinations. The statements all refer to a proposal in Congress to place a high import tax on Japanese cars, electronic parts, and textile goods.

(1) "This would be a sure way to start a *trade war* with the Japanese, who would retaliate by enacting tariffs against American goods, which would throw American factory *workers out of jobs*."

(2) "This might start a *trade war* with the Japanese, who could retaliate by erecting tariff barriers against American manufactured goods, which would throw American factory *workers out of work*."

(3) "This might help *protect American workers* against competition with cheap foreign labor."

(4) "This is the only effective way to keep the wages of American factory *workers* up where they should be!"

OR

(1) "If you want to raise prices to the American *consumers* while protecting the profits of large American corporations, this is the best way to do it!"

(2) "There is a real possibility that this would raise prices to the American *consumer* while protecting the profits of some large, inefficient corporations."

(3) "This would help to protect certain militarily *strategic* American industries against extinction!"

(4) "This is a necessary and effective move if we want to protect certain militarily *strategic* American industries from extinction!"

These eight items were constructed from imagination, without benefit of the various discovery processes outlined earlier. Therefore, the items might possibly prove to be unscalable, not because the ordinal end-means calibration was not built in but because in so doing end-means issues may have been brought in which are not actually attitude-supporting themes in the population to be tested. For example, the first set of four items would represent ordinal positions on a scale only if all respondents assumed that protecting American *workers* is a good end. Only then would the proposed import tax be judged consistently in terms of its probable effectiveness as a means to this end.

However, the proposed import tax could be judged in terms of its probable effects on other ends, such the welfare of the American *consumer* or American *industry*, as shown in the second set of four items. If none of these ends has become involved in the emotional-polarization process during public discussion of the import-tax issue, then the statements, instead of eliciting an attitudinally determined response, only invite the respondent to ask himself, "What is the actual cause-and-effect relationship involved?" Since most respondents would not have the knowledge required, they would be forced to take a neutral position in responding to each statement.

It does not matter whether a person's arguments are determined by his attitude or his attitude is determined by his arguments as long as the anti attitudes are connected to one set of arguments and the pro attitudes are connected to another set of arguments. If there is a strong attitude, the respondent will welcome an argument supporting his conclusion even though he cannot prove it to be factually correct.

Thus far we have described three types of *essence* themes: the *criteria of judgment* theme, the *mutability* theme, and the *end-means* theme. We illustrated how sets of items can be constructed on each theme to give the set a calibration in terms of ordinal position on the attitude scale.

The next set of themes we will explore all refer to the *interaction* between the object of the attitude and the respondent or his in-group. Of course, this aspect of an attitude is closely related to the essence aspect, because we often explain or rationalize our preferred form of interaction with an object in terms of our perception of the essential nature of that object.

Interaction Themes.   The particular types of interaction themes described here are not the only ones nor necessarily the best ones that can be devised. They may appear to be commonsensical; however, they were inductively derived from many examples of attitude scales constructed by the writer, other social scientists, and students in methodology courses.

The contact theme refers to the degree to which the respondent prefers to seek versus avoid, or accept versus reject, the object of his attitude. The Bogardus Social-Distance scale is one of the earliest examples of the systematic use of this theme. As has been shown in Figure 12, he used a scale of seven items representing different degrees of intimacy of relationship. Note that all seven of the social-distance categories are in the fourth-facet form (*hypothetical action*) since the instructions say to "mark an 'X' after each of the relation-

Indicate which relationships you would be willing to have with each of the groups listed. Do not give your reactions to the best or the worst members you have known, but think of the picture or stereo-type that you have of the whole group. In each column make an "X" after each of the relationships to which *you would be willing* to admit a member of that group.

	English	Swedes	Poles	Mexican	Koreans
(1) To close kin-ship by marriage.					
(2) To my club as a personal friend.					
(3) To my street as a neighbor.					
(4) To employment in my occupa-tion.					
(5) To citizenship in my country.					
(6) As a visitor only to my country.					
(7) Would exclude from my country.					

Figure 12. *Bogardus Social-Distance Scale Format*

ships to which you would be willing to admit a member of that group." Also, the form of response is an "all or none" dichotomy rather than a five-point scale as in Likert and some Guttman items. Therefore, the Bogardus scale must obtain its ordinal calibration ex-clusively from the nature of the content, with no variation at the facet or response-category level.

The social-distance theme is a specific example of a contact theme. The seven items derive their calibration from the fact that they cor-relate with degrees of social intimacy, with probable frequency of contact, and with degrees of social equality. Other scales based on the contact theme could make more direct use of the frequency-of-contact idea. This is illustrated in the Frequency of Contact Scale example (Figure 13). Since the eleven categories are obviously arranged in a quantitative order, it is necessary for the respondent to check only one item in each column. As in the Bogardus scale, the calibration of the total scale depends completely upon the content of the items.

The specific items used to measure the contact-avoidance dimension depend upon the object of contact or avoidance. In the Bogardus example the object was an ethnic or nationality group. In the Frequency-of-Contact Scale example the object is a family member. The idea of contact-avoidance could also be applied to rock and roll music, radicals, lectures on U.S. history, or California weather.

In *sanction* themes we define *sanctions* as any form of reward or punishment of the object of the attitude regardless of whether or not the action is based on legitimate authority. If the object is a person or group of persons, the sanction can be applied directly. If the object is a form of action, policy, or thought, then the reward or punishment is given to those who agree or disagree with such action, policy, or thought. This theme is more easily applied when the object is a group or category of people distinguished by a particular form of behavior, as illustrated in the nine-item Sanction-Theme Scale shown in Figure 14.

This particular set of items proved to be a very good scale according to Guttman criteria. It is highly probable that attitudes toward male homosexuals could just as well have been measured by a set of items based on the contact theme. In this case the items would simply range from statements showing preference or tolerance to avoidance of male homosexuals.

The sanction theme probably lends itself more readily to measuring attitudes of people who are extremely anti or extremely pro, while the social-contact theme is probably able to make finer gradations for people in the middle of the attitude range—those who feel that homosexuals should be neither rewarded nor punished but simply recognized as having a distinctive way of life (a subculture). In this case the attitude is manifested in terms of differences in social status between the respondent's and the homosexual's ways of life, or in terms of the degree of contact with the other way of life preferred by the respondent. Therefore, it is likely that a more sensitive scale could have been constructed using *both* sanction themes and contact themes, in which case the continuum would look something like this:

Punish	Avoid	Tolerate	Seek out	Reward
Anti				Pro

Figure 13. *Frequency-of-Contact Scale*

For each person listed below please indicate what you feel would be the ideal frequency of contact between you and that person in your own home. Put one "X" in each column to indicate the ideal frequency.

	Husband or Wife	Brother or Sister	Mother or Father	Grandmother or Grandfather	Mother-in-Law or Father-in-Law
(1) Several times per day					
(2) At least once per day					
(3) Three or four times per week					
(4) At least once per week					
(5) Three or four times per month					
(6) At least once per month					
(7) Six to ten times per year					
(8) Three to five times per year					
(9) Two or three times per year					
(10) Only once per year					
(11) Less than once per year					

Homosexual relations between two consenting adult males should be dealt with in which of the following ways? Respond to each statement using the following key:

1–Strongly disagree   4–Agree
2–Disagree   5–Strongly agree
3–Not sure

——(a) "They should be punished by execution."
——(b) "They should serve at least five years in prison."
——(c) "They should be given a short prison sentence."
——(d) "They should be required to accept treatment or go to jail."
——(e) "They should be offered treatment if they want it but not punished in any way, but warned not to recruit younger boys into homosexuality."
——(f) "They should not be made to feel deviant or warned about recruiting younger boys."
——(g) "They should be praised for choosing their own form of sexual satisfaction as long as it does not interfere with those who prefer heterosexuality."
——(h) "They should be praised and encouraged to recruit young boys into homosexuality."

Figure 14. *Sanction-Theme Scale*

This design should give a wider range of scores, make finer distinctions between attitudes, and avoid many tied scores. Even the sanction-theme items could be expanded to include statements indicating degrees of social ostracism instead of jumping from legal sanctions of jail and fines in items (a) through (d) to the therapy item (e). Such a range might include statements like the following:

"They should not be allowed to hold such jobs as public school teacher or minister."

"They should not have a job as a YMCA staff member."

"They should not be allowed in the Army."

One could even add some items lifted directly from the Bogardus Social-Distance scale, such as the following:

"I wouldn't want them to be a member of a *club* I belonged to."

"I wouldn't want them to live in my *neighborhood.*"

"I wouldn't want them to *work* at the same place I do."

By *sentiment* themes we simply mean statements that could fall along a continuum such as love-hate, like-dislike, accept-reject, attraction-repulsion, or amity-hostility. These bipolar pairs may sound very similar to the pairs falling into both the contact themes and sanction themes which we have just discussed. The affinity is based on the fact that the three themes depict different modes of manifesting the same attitude. For example, we tend to seek out (contact) and reward (sanction) whatever we love (sentiment), and we tend to avoid and punish whatever we hate.

The distinction among the three themes is not an idle academic exercise; each theme is useful in sensitizing us to a variety of statements when we are trying to discover, select, or construct attitude items. In reality, a set of statements can be a mixture of all three themes, since we are striving not to have pure types of statements but to have a number of statements which fall at different points on the same continuum.

Figure 15 is an example of the use of pure sentiment-theme statements. In their pure form, these seven statements might appear too obvious to the respondents or might fail to elicit attitudinal responses because respondents might take refuge in the "undecided" answer category since they do not know for certain how "most Anglos" think. This possibility can be reduced by (a) prefacing each statement with "I think" or "I believe," or explaining in the directions that the respondent is to indicate how he *believes* most Anglos feel; or (b) expressing the different degrees of hate or love in terms of actions that should be taken toward Chicanos by the community.

Treatment (b) can be amplified by expressing the action statements in at least two facet-forms: the moral imperative form ("what should be done") and the hypothetical-action form ("what I would do"). To elicit responses from those holding the more extreme attitudes, some of the statements could be transformed from the social-stereotype form ("Most Anglos have a strong feeling . . .") to the personal-belief form ("I have a strong feeling . . ."). The main point is that attitude statements can be made up of direct or indirect declarations of sentiment as distinct from the contact-theme or sanction-theme approach.

In discussing types of content themes, we began by dividing content-of-attitude statements into two aspects: essence themes and interaction themes. Among the suggested essence themes were (a) the criteria-of-judgment theme (morality, legality, practicality), (b) the ends-means theme, and (c) the mutability theme. Among the interaction themes were (a) the contact themes, (b) the sanction theme, and (c) the sentiment theme. We have illustrated how in some cases an ordinal metric can be built into a set of items using themes at the content level alone without relying on different facet forms or the response patterns for the metric.

There has been a lot of discussion in the newspapers lately about relations between Anglos and Chicanos here in San Fernando. Please indicate the extent to which you agree or disagree with each of the statements below, using the following key:

     1-Strongly agree
     2-Agree
     3-Undecided
     4-Disagree
     5-Strongly disagree

——(a) "Most Anglos here have a *strong hatred* for the Chicanos."
——(b) "Most Anglos here have a *clear dislike* for most Chicanos."
——(c) "Most Anglos here have *some feeling against* Chicanos."
——(d) "Most Anglos here have *nothing against* the Chicanos."
——(e) "Most Anglos here have *some feeling in favor* of Chicanos."
——(f) "Most Anglos here have a *clear feeling in favor* of Chicanos."
——(g) "Most Anglos here have a *strong love* for Chicanos."

Figure 15. *Sentiment-Theme Scale*

LABORATORY PROBLEM 2
Recognizing Content Themes

Below are twenty additional statements on the same topic used in Laboratory Problem 1. This illustrates how an almost endless variety of statements can be found related to a topic. Several valid attitude scales could be constructed without ever repeating the same item. Here your task is simply to identify the type of content theme represented by each of these twenty statements. Use the following key.

Key

     1-Contact theme
     2-Sanction theme
     3-Criterion of judgment
     4-Ends-means relationship
     5-Sentiment theme
     6-Mutability theme

—— (1) "I feel good when I think of the SWP."
—— (2) "The SWP is full of good ideals but completely ineffective."
—— (3) "The SWP is a basically hypocritical organization."

___ (4) "The SWP is becoming less negative and more thoughtfully positive lately."

___ (5) "I wouldn't marry anyone who was not a SWP member."

___ (6) "I wouldn't want an SWP member as a roommate."

___ (7) "The SWP is a very good political organization."

___ (8) "The SWP should not be allowed to organize on American college campuses."

___ (9) "The SWP is a very effective organization for radicalizing students."

___(10) "I feel threatened by the SWP as a political organization."

___(11) "I would like to have SWP members as students on this campus."

___(12) "I frankly believe that the aims of the SWP would be detrimental to society."

___(13) "The national leaders of SWP deserve praise and recognition for their work."

___(14) "The SWP is very effective in a destructive sort of way."

___(15) "I don't want to be bothered with talking to SWP members."

___(16) "I would feel bad if the SWP became a potent force on the campus."

___(17) "The leaders of SWP are very efficient in organizing for constructive change."

___(18) "The SWP is basically an autocratic type of organization."

___(19) "Contributions to the SWP should be deductible for income-tax purposes."

___(20) "I don't think members of the SWP should be allowed in the United States."

Facets as Calibration

We introduced the concept of facets in our illustrations of the three-level calibration and showed how a content-theme statement may be divided into two or more facet forms which can be put into ordinal position on the scale. In this compact example we did not explain the rationale behind the facet metric.

What we have called "facets" for simplicity Guttman[8] sees as a combination of three components.

(A) Subject's Behavior
   a_1 = belief
   a_2 = overt action

[8] Louis Guttman, "A Structural Theory for Intergroup Beliefs and Action," *American Sociological Review* 24, No. 3 (June, 1959): 318–28.

Facet Combination	Components
(1) Stereotype	$a_1 \ b_1 \ c_1$
(2) Norm	$a_1 \ b_1 \ c_2$
(3) Hypothetical interaction	$a_1 \ b_2 \ c_2$
(4) Personal interaction	$a_2 \ b_2 \ c_2$

Figure 16. *Facet Combinations and Their Components*

    (B) Referent
        b_1 = subject's group
        b_2 = subject himself
    (C) Referent's Intergroup Behavior
        c_1 = comparative
        c_2 = interactive

Since each of the three components offers two possible types of statements, it would be possible to obtain eight ($2 \times 2 \times 2 = 8$) different combinations. Guttman selects four of the eight combinations as the most clearly scalable, as shown in Figure 16.

The assumption underlying the assignment of ordinal positions to the four facet combinations is that the implied continuum in each of the three facet dimensions is the degree of *ego involvement*. It is assumed that overt action is a more ego-involved expression of attitude than is mere belief. Thus, a person who acts on an issue feels more strongly than one who believes but does not act. Similarly, it is assumed that if a person attributes an attitude to his in-group this is less ego-involved than if he claims the attitude to be his own. Finally, it is assumed that comparing another group unfavorably with one's in-group is a less forceful manifestation of attitude than acting toward members of the out-group in an unfavorable way.

As we progress from facet (1) to (4), each combination of components contains one additional subscript ("2"), indicating additional ego-involvement. Guttman's article shows how he statistically tested this assumption of ordinal position.

Jordan[9] refines the four facet combinations into six by dividing the "norm" facet into two, distinguishing between the "societal norm" and the "personal norm," and by splitting "personal interaction" into "interacting symbolically" and "interacting operationally."

In my five-facet combinations, I accepted Jordan's first distinction as useful, but I have found the second distinction too difficult to

[9] J. E. Jordan, "A Guttman Facet Theory Analysis of Teacher Attitudes Toward the Mentally Retarded in Colombia, British Honduras, and the United States," *Indian Journal of Mental Retardation* 3 (1970): 1–20.

make reliably in scale construction. My five-facet set is not precisely translatable into the Guttman and Jordan categories, but it is clearly derived in principle from them. These five facets were illustrated earlier in Figure 10, page 56, and Laboratory Problem 3 provides practice in recognizing them.

LABORATORY PROBLEM 3
Recognizing Facet-Types

Below are twenty statements related to a variety of attitudes and representing five different facet-types. If you can recognize each type as it occurs in statements about different objects of attitude, it will help toward the more creative step of constructing your own statements.

Classify each statement according to the facet-type using the following key.

Key

1–Societal stereotype
2–Personal belief
3–Moral imperative
4–Hypothetical action
5–Real personal action

—— (1) "I have refused to register for the draft."
—— (2) "If I were approached by a homosexual I would really tell him off."
—— (3) "Heroin pushers should be immediately apprehended and put in jail."
—— (4) "I feel that blacks can be trusted with money as much as whites."
—— (5) "Everyone knows that the use of heroin is a social evil."
—— (6) "Most people know that homosexuals are peculiar in many ways."
—— (7) "I turned in a heroin pusher that I learned about."
—— (8) "I feel that heroin is a serious menace to society."
—— (9) "I would go to jail before I would join the Army."
——(10) "All homosexuals should be put in jail."
——(11) "Most people don't like people of another race."
——(12) "It is clear to me that homosexuals need our sympathy."
——(13) "All men should refuse to fight on another country's soil."
——(14) "If anyone tried to sell heroin to me I'd turn them in to the police."

___(15) "I have told homosexuals that they should have a right to do their own thing."

___(16) "I have refused to loan money to blacks at work."

___(17) "The majority of Americans feel that the United States should not send troops abroad."

___(18) "If a black were to ask me for a loan I wouldn't give it to him."

___(19) "I feel that the Vietnam War was immoral."

___(20) "It is wrong to trust blacks with money."

Response Forms as Calibration

Several forms of responses to questions or statements have a built-in ordinal calibration. The early attitude scales by Bogardus and Thurstone had no refined ca¹ibration built into the response itself. In both cases the respondent was allowed only to accept or reject a statement, to agree or disagree with a statement, or to say "yes" or "no" to a question. Likert and others showed several ways to escape the limitations of the dichotomous answer which fails to register finer distinctions of attitude.

Listed below are seven different response forms which can be used under many circumstances.

Amount of Agreement. When the attitude item is in the form of a statement, the answer can be structured in terms of degrees of agreement or disagreement. For example:

___Strongly disagree
___Disagree
___Neutral (not sure, undecided)
___Agree
___Strongly agree

In some cases this five-point answer can be reduced to three by eliminating the two extremes.

Comparative Responses. When the attitude question or statement is put in a form requiring the respondent to compare his own group with the out-group toward which his attitude is being measured, the responses are structured as completions of comparative statements. For example: "Whites help their neighbors. . .

___less often than blacks."
___about as often as blacks."
___more often than blacks."

Predictions of Action. When the attitude item is in the form of a hypothetical action statement, the response may take the form illustrated:

"What would you do it you were offered some grass to smoke at a party?"

___(1) I'm sure I would refuse it.
___(2) I would probably refuse it.
___(3) I'm not sure what I would do.
___(4) I would probably accept it.
___(5) I'm sure I would accept it.

Predictions of Feelings. If the attitude item is in the form of a statement or question about the respondent's feeling toward the object of attitude, the response is structured very similarly to the previous one. For example:

"How do you feel when you hear jokes putting down women drivers?"

___(1) Very disgusted.
___(2) Don't like it.
___(3) Indifferent.
___(4) It's funny.
___(5) Very funny.

Reporting of Own Actions. If the attitude item deals with the overt interaction facet, the response categories can ask for the frequency of certain interactions. For example:

"About how often, on the average, do you talk to white students?"

___(1) Several times per day.
___(2) Two or three times per day.
___(3) At least once per day.
___(4) Several times per week.
___(5) Three or four times per week.
___(6) At least once per week.
___(7) Less than once per week.
___(8) Less than once per month.

Threshold of Reaction. One way of registering degrees of attitude toward an object is in terms of the respondents' sensitivity to the presence of the object. This sensitivity can be expressed in terms of the amount of the attitudinal object required to elicit a reaction. The more anti the person is to the object, the less of the object is needed to trigger a reaction. For example:

"I think the College should organize a strong effort to deal with the hard-drug problem . . .

——(1) even if we don't yet have any users on campus."
——(2) if there is evidence of a single user on the campus."
——(3) if as many as 1% of the students and faculty are users."
——(4) if 5% or more of the students and faculty are users."
——(5) if 10% or more of the students and faculty are users."

Strength of Response.   When the stimulus object is clear and there is general agreement that "something should be done about it," it is possible to register degrees of attitude by allowing responses which indicate different strengths of response toward the stimulus object. For example:

"If I felt that it would be successful in getting the government to take strong action against pollution of air and water, I would be willing to. . .

——(1) sign a petition to my senator."
——(2) write a postcard to my senator."
——(3) write a long letter to my senator."
——(4) take a petition around to be signed."
——(5) take around a petition and urge others to write their congressman."

These examples do not include all the possible ways of quantifying responses, but they should suggest a variety of scalable response patterns allowing us to use a variety of forms of questions and statements.

In the preceding section I have tried to give some useful suggestions for the discovery, selection, and calibration of a set of attitude items that will have a chance of approximating unidimensionality, will cover the full range of attitudes, and will be calibrated finely enough to provide a sensitive measuring instrument. In explaining the next phase of the process I assume that a set of items has been discovered, selected, and constructed and are ready to be administered to the people whose attitudes are being measured. I will show the rationale, methods, and techniques for testing, measuring, and improving the scalability of the set of items. Even by applying the guidelines offered for constructing relevant and scalable items, we cannot expect to have a perfect scale without doing some modification after the questionnaire is administered. These modifications are part of the Guttman scaling method.

Laboratory Problem 4 provides an opportunity to apply two levels of calibration (content-theme and facet) simultaneously in judging the scale order of a set of items.

LABORATORY PROBLEM 4

Predicting Scale Order of Items

In the ten statements below, the scale order depends upon the content-theme metric and the facet metric. Since the response categories are omitted, no response-form metric is involved. You are to attempt to arrange the ten items in rank order according to your prediction of their scale position. Of course, in reality the scale positions would be determined by the relative frequency of positive responses from the sample of respondents. However, there is always a high correlation between the order predicted by a number of competent judges and the actual order shown in the subsequent scalogram analysis. If there is little agreement among independent judges on the scale position of an item, this may be due to some ambiguity of meaning which you might uncover in discussing your disagreements with others.

Procedure:

   (a) Put a + or – sign in front of each statement to indicate whether the statement is *pro* or *anti* atheism.
   (b) Determine which *pro* statement seems the *strongest*, the *weakest*, and then the order of the remaining pro statements in between.
   (c) Repeat step (b) with the *anti* statements.
   (d) Number the items from 1 to 10, using 1 for the most *anti* statement.
   (e) Now read through all ten statements to check whether they still seem to be in rank order.

___ (1) "All atheists should be thrown in jail and have their property confiscated."
___ (2) "Atheists should not be allowed to teach in public schools or universities."
___ (3) "The churches should make a concerted effort to expose the fallacies of atheism."
___ (4) "Tolerance of atheism is an important element in democracy."
___ (5) "I feel that atheism is a very sensible philosophical position."

—— (6) "Only atheists should be allowed to hold government jobs so that they won't have a conflicting loyalty to religion."

—— (7) "Atheists should not be allowed to send their literature through the U.S. mails."

—— (8) "We might have to tolerate atheism but we shouldn't be deceived by it."

—— (9) "I enjoy the stimulation of discussion with an intelligent atheist."

——(10) "Atheists should receive public recognition for their contribution to philosophical thought."

Chapter 3. Designing and Administering the Scale

Once we have succeeded in discovering, selecting, and constructing a number of individual questions or statements and their response categories, we can turn to the problems of questionnaire design.

DESIGNING THE SCALE

Several decisions must be made about how to combine the individual items into one instrument to be used as a questionnaire or interview schedule. How many items should be included? In what order should the items appear? Should the same number of response categories be used for all of the statements? Should masking items be added to obscure the unidimensional intent of the scale items? What format should be used, and how will this affect editing, coding, or the use of electronic data-processing methods?

How Many Items Should Be Included?

We must distinguish between the number of items required in the finished or purified scale and the number used in the original questionnair. First, let's consider the number of items needed in the purified scale.

There is no magic number of items we can specify as adequate to do the job. In theory a scale can have as few as three items or as many as 100. In most practical applications of scaling the number of items ranges between 5 and 25. To determine the number of items needed, several factors must be considered simultaneously, including scale sensitivity, validity, and data processing.

Scale Sensitivity. The number of items in the scale affects its sensitivity or the fineness of the distinctions the scale will make between one respondent and another. For example, if a scale has three items with trichotomous answers, and the three answer categories are given the values of 0, 1, and 2, the range of possible total scores will be from 0 to 6. If there are 10 such trichotomous items, the range will be from 0 to 20. If we assume that both sets of items actually cover the full range of attitude from extreme pro to extreme anti, then the difference between them is in the number of distinctions they can make.

In the case of the 0-to-6 range, in any typical population there is a high probability that about 80% of the cases will have scores of 2, 3, or 4 since 0 and 1, along with 5 and 6, represent the extreme attitudes. Whether or not this is a fine enough distinction depends upon how the scores are to be used. For example, if we intend to measure the association between attitude score and the trichotomous attribute of political affiliation (Democrat, Republican, Independent), we could trichotomize attitude scores into anti, neutral, and pro to produce the contingency table shown in Figure 17 and proceed to measure the amount of association using Tschuprow's T^2 and the amount of statistical significance with X^2 (Chi square).

It would be of little value to use more items (which results in a more refined scale) and then throw the scores into three class intervals if the only gain associated with an increase in the number of items were an increase in sensitivity of the scale. However, as we will see later, there are other advantages to increasing the number of items. Also, it is important to note that the sensitivity of a scale can be increased not only by increasing the number of items but also by increasing the number of response categories to each item. For example, five dichotomous items give a range of 0 to 5, five trichotomous

Figure 17. *Frequency Distribution of 1000 Registered Voters in Browne County, Indiana, by Political Affiliation and Attitude Toward Welfare Recipients*

		Attitude			
		LOW (0, 1, 2) Anti	MEDIUM (3) Neutral	HIGH (4, 5, 6) Pro	Totals
Political Affiliation	Democrat	40	310	250	600
	Republican	200	75	75	350
	Independent	10	15	25	50
	Totals	250	400	350	1000

items give a range of 0 to 10, and five items with five answer categories produce a maximum range of 0 to 20.

If we want to use the attitude scores to do a rank correlation with another attitude scale, at least 10 items should be used in order to have as many different scores as possible. (When two people tie for the same score, they must also be given the same rank value on that variable. If there are too many ties, the Spearman Rank Correlation is invalid, for statistical reasons we will not explore here.) Of course, if the respondents in a particular sample all cluster in a small portion of the range of the scale, then the number of tie scores will increase. For this reason it would be safer to have 25 items in the scale.

Thus, it is clear that when the scores are to be used in rank correlation, we must have a scale that makes many distinctions of degree; but in the case of the contingency-table analysis, it would be undesirable to make a more highly refined scale if it were not for validity considerations.

Scale Validity.   It can be shown that in general the more items there are in a scale (of a given level of *reproducibility*, which will be explained later), the greater the assurance that the items validly belong to the same dimension rather than being included by chance.[1] A larger number of items assures us that there is a smaller probability that each item was included in the set because of chance factors and a greater probability that each item was included because it shares the common property which defines the dimension. This relationship between the number of items and validity of the reproducibility has been demonstrated by Green and others.

It can also be shown that increasing the number of response categories makes a higher degree of validity possible. However, increasing the number of items or response categories does not automatically ensure greater validity. It is more precise to say that if two scales have the same coefficient of reproducibility, the one with the larger number of items or response categories will be the more valid.

Electronic Data Processing.   There are some limits to the number of items that can be included in a scale if we want to use the readily available electronic data-processing programs for Guttman scaling. One of the best explanations of the programing of Guttman scale data[2] offers a program with the following limitations:

(1) No more than 100 different items may be included in the total bank of information to be processed.

[1] For example, see Green's formula for reproducibility (unidimensionality) in Gary M. Maranell (ed.), *Scaling: A Sourcebook for Behavioral Scientists* (Chicago: Aldine Publishing Co., 1974), pp. 183–85.

[2] Norman H. Nie, Dale H. Bent, and C. Hadlai Hull, *Statistical Package for the Social Sciences* (New York: McGraw-Hill Book Co., 1970), p. 205.

(2) Any 12 of these 100 items may be considered and tested jointly for their scalability.
(3) No more than four response categories may be used for any item.
(4) Up to 50 sets of 12 items each can be tested for scalability in one program.

The electronic data processing performs a modern miracle by simultaneously testing the scalability of any 50 different combinations of 12 items we wish to select from the pool of 100 items. But a most serious limitation is that it will yield a scale of no more than 12 items and no more than four response categories each. This means that the maximum range of scores would be 0 to 36 if the answer categories have the values of 0, 1, 2, 3. If this is too restricting for a particular purpose, we could use electronic data processing to do the preliminary selection from a larger number of items, which could then be tested for their coefficient of reproducibility by the scalogram technique to be described in the next chapter.

It is important to note at this point that electronic data processing cannot produce a scale from any combination of items unless we have first been successful in discovering, selecting, and constructing a majority of items that fall on a single dimension. If the initial items are not scalable, the scaling program will quickly demonstrate in the print-outs that none of the combinations of 12 items fulfills the criterion of scalability and that the data-collection effort was wasted.

Scalogram Analysis. If we analyze the data without electronic data processing it is more important to keep the number of items relatively small. The process becomes too complicated when the number of items gets above 15. This is particularly true if more than one out of ten items must be rejected. This is another reason for putting considerable effort into the discovery, selection, and construction of valid items. I have been most successful when using an initial set of 10 to 20 items and retaining 8 to 17 items in the final purified scale.

No matter how convinced we are that the initial set of items is good, it is a wise precaution to have a few more items than are needed in the final scale to assure the range, sensitivity, and validity required, because there is always a loss of sensitivity (range of scores) through the rejection of items, collapsing of response categories, or both.

In What Order Should the Items Appear?

Regardless of the order in which the items are put in the questionnaire, the researcher should have a clear idea of the scale order of the items. If in using the scale with a given sample of a population we find that the items do indeed fall in the predicted order, this gives added credence to the validity of the scale. However, if the items appear in the questionnaire in rank order from most anti to most pro statements, it becomes obvious to the respondent that he or she is dealing with a measuring instrument rather than with a set of unrelated opinion items. Whether this awareness will increase or decrease the reliability and validity of the response depends upon whether the awareness constitutes an ego-threat under the circumstances.[3] If the subject matter is not controversial, if the respondent's answers are completely anonymous, or if there is no other danger of ego-threat, then it would be more convenient to put the items in order from the most anti to the most pro or vice versa. In some instances researchers have made two forms of the questionnaire in which the items are arranged in opposite rank orders in case the order provided a context to bias the responses.

If a scalogram sheet is used in testing the reproducibility, it is more esthetically pleasing to see the response patterns when the items are placed in rank order on the scale, but this is not necessary for calculating the coefficient of reproducibility using either the scalogram or electronic data-processing program.

Should Masking Items Be Included?

Under some circumstances it is possible to obtain more candid and spontaneous responses to attitude items if the respondents are not aware of the particular attitude being measured. In this situation 15 or 20 items belonging to the scale may be interspersed with 20 to 40 items on a wider range of topics. The whole questionnaire may be introduced as "a chance to give your opinions on a number of topics."

Certain cautions must be observed if masking items are used. First, they should not form a context which will tend to bias responses to the scale items. Second, the number and complexity of the items should not make the whole questionnaire so long that fatigue begins to distort the responses near the end of the questionnaire or the refusal rate is increased.

Unless there is a convincing reason to include masking items they should be omitted to avoid complications and inefficiency in the collection and analysis of the data.

---

[3] A conceptualization of the conditions of ego-threat in information gathering is found throughout the following volume: Raymond L. Gorden, *Interviewing: Strategy, Techniques and Tactics* (Homewood, Ill.: Dorsey Press, 1975).

How Many Response Categories Should Be Used?

There is no need to have the same number of response categories for every item. The Guttman technique can handle a mixture of response types from the simple dichotomous up to any number. However, there are studies showing that most respondents fail to make any reliable distinctions beyond seven points. Even five-point distinctions often prove to be unreliable according to Guttman-scale criteria. The general practice has developed to limit the response range to a five-point maximum. We must still be prepared to collapse two or three categories into one after seeing the response patterns in the scalogram. This collapsing operation will be discussed in detail later.

There are good reasons for using a five-point response scale even though some of the response categories may later have to be combined so that there are only two or three categories in the final scoring of the questionnaire. First, respondents who resent having to give a dichotomous (forced choice) response to an opinion or attitude item do not object if they are given a five-point latitude. Second, in any item where the finer distinctions prove to be reliable, all the original categories may be retained; this yields a wider range of scores than does using only dichotomous items.

In some cases the number of response categories is automatically determined by the nature of the statement. For example, the following questions all imply a dichotomous response structure with a residual third category such as "the same" or "neither":

(a) "Do you feel that whites or blacks look more alike?"
(b) "Did you vote for Nixon or McGovern in 1972?"
(c) "Do you think that North Vietnam or South Vietnam lost most in that struggle?"

Of course some items can be converted from a dichotomous form to a five-point response simply by rewording the question or converting it to a statement. For example, question (a) above could be converted into a statement with a five-point response as follows:

"Blacks look much more alike than do whites."

____(1) Strongly agree
____(2) Agree
____(3) Don't know
____(4) Disagree
____(5) Strongly disagree

No such conversion is appropriate with question (b), which refers to an action in which there were only two choices for the voters. We could ask a related question, "How sure do you feel now that you voted for the right person," and give a five-point response, but that would be quite a different question.

No technical problem results if the number of response categories varies from one item to another, so a fairly safe rule is to use dichotomous or trichotomous response categories when the nature of item demands it and a five-point response scale whenever possible.

What Format Should Be Used?

In deciding on the format of the questionnaire, we are faced with such choices as whether we should use one response key at the top of the page as in Format A (Figure 18), or provide a different set of response categories after each item as in Format B (Figure 19), or repeat the same set of response categories for each item as in Format C (Figure 20). In comparing these three formats it is immediately apparent that A and C can be used only if the same number of responses is appropriate for all the items in the questionnaire, including any masking items that might be used. Format A has the advantage of allowing more items on a page since less space is taken up with the answer categories. With this format, if all the items cannot be put on a single page, the response key should be repeated at the top of each page.

An essential difference between Formats A and B is in the scoring. In A it is necessary to transform some of the response code numbers from 1 to 5 and 5 to 1, as well as to transform some from 2 to 4, or 4 to 2. This must be done so that answers 1 through 5 will always correspond to a consistent *direction* of attitude. If we want the high score in this example to indicate strong fear of assault, then the response "strongly agree" should have a value of 5 in item (a) and a value of 1 in item (b) and a value of 5 in item (c). Without this transformation it would make no sense to add up the response codes to obtain a total score.

In Format C this transformation step can be avoided by the appropriate construction of the format. Note that in items (a) and (b) "strongly agree" is on the left while in item (c) it is on the right. Thus it is a simple operation to assign a value of 5 to every check on the extreme left and a value of 1 to every check on the extreme right and the values of the columns in between become 4, 3, 2 from left to right.[4]

---

[4] Although no transforming of numbers is involved in Format C, it is necessary for the coder to write the appropriate scale value of the response in front of the item number for every item.

Please show how much your opinion agrees or disagrees with each
of the statements below by using the following key:

> 1-Strongly agree
> 2-Agree
> 3-Undecided or neutral
> 4-Disagree
> 5-Strongly disagree

——(a) One shouldn't walk downtown alone at night.
——(b) It is perfectly safe to walk downtown alone at night.
——(c) There is reason to fear possible assault even in this small
        town.

Figure 18. *Format A Response*

Please show how much you agree or disagree with each of the statements below by checking the most appropriate blank after each
item.

(a) One shouldn't walk downtown alone at night.
    ——(4) Strongly agree
    ——(3) Agree
    ——(2) Undecided
    ——(1) Disagree
    ——(0) Strongly disagree

(b) The college should arrange to increase police protection.
    ——(2) Immediately!
    ——(1) If any more assaults on students occur.
    ——(0) Not unless there is an increase in the assault rate.

Figure 19. *Format B Response*

If either the *number* of responses or the *names* of the categories
vary from one item to another, then we cannot use Format A. If
there is a uniform number of response categories but their names
change from item to item, it would be possible to use Format C but
not A. In this case, if the names of all the categories are short enough
or if fine print can be used, then the horizontal continuum could be
used as in Format C, but if the names are too long then they must be
listed vertically, as in Format B.

Format B has the widest range of applicability since it can be used
in those cases where A and C apply as well as in cases where they
cannot. In Format B the number of response categories need not be

Please show how much you agree or disagree with each of the statements below by checking the most appropriate category after each item.

(a) Students should *not* walk alone at night downtown.
——Strongly agree
——Agree
——Neutral
——Disagree
——Strongly disagree

(b) There is reason to fear possible assault even in this small town.
——Strongly agree
——Agree
——Neutral
——Disagree
——Strongly disagree

(c) The danger of being assaulted at night has greatly subsided and there is no longer any reason to worry about it.
——Strongly disagree
——Disagree
——Neutral
——Disagree
——Strongly agree

Figure 20. *Format C Response*

uniform from item to item and the names of the categories may be either short or long. Note that in Format B the scale values are contained in the parentheses so that, in effect, the respondent checks the appropriate scale value as he checks the verbal response category. The only disadvantage in using Format B is that it will often require two pages to contain the same number of items that could be put on one page with Formats A or C. The importance of this consideration varies with the particular data-gathering situation, including such variables as the number of respondents, whether the questionnaire is to be mailed, and the amount of skill, experience, and knowledge of the coders.

We have found no experimental studies establishing the relative reliability or intelligibility of the three formats used in connection with the same set of items. It appears that all three are quite adequate as long as the format in each case makes it clear which response categories are meaningful to the respondent.

Any of the three formats can be adapted to electronic data processing if a large number of respondents—over 500, for example—is required. The most practical is the mark-sense input system. In this process the respondent indicates his choice or response by filling in the space between two parallel dotted lines with a special electrographic pencil. The machine can be programmed to assign the appropriate scale value to each response and to reject cases with missing responses.

What Instructions Should Be Given to the Respondent?

Whether or not written instructions to the respondent are included as part of the questionnaire format depends upon whether or not the researcher is to be present. Regardless of whether the instructions to the respondents are to be written or oral, a few important points should be included in language appropriate to the respondents. If the responses are to be anonymous, this should be made clear to the respondents. Also, it should be indicated that there are no "right" or "wrong" answers but that the items are matters of personal opinion. Therefore, the respondents should be urged to give their most spontaneous reaction rather than to study the items to find some logical clue to the answers. Below are some sample instructions taken from various scale questionnaires.

> "This is not a test. There are no right or wrong answers. All of the items below are matters of opinion, so give your initial reaction quickly without wasting time looking for some logical clues to answers. Just choose the answer that comes closest to expressing your opinion on the matter."

> "This is an opinion poll to show the range of ideas people have on current events. There are no factual questions with right or wrong answers, so work rapidly to give your most spontaneous reaction to each item. Your answers are anonymous and will be used for statistical purposes only. So let yourself go!"

> "This opinionnaire contains a wide range of statements different people have made about the women's liberation movement. In each item quickly pick out the answer category that comes closest to your own opinion on the matter. There are no right or wrong answers in a factual sense, and your answers will be kept anonymous and used for statistical purposes only. Work rapidly and be spontaneous."

Whether such instructions are written or oral (or both) depends upon the situation in which the questionnaire is being administered.

At this point, before going on to the scalogram analysis process, you should take time to develop your own set of attitude scale items. Laboratory Problem 5 summarizes the procedure for this.

LABORATORY PROBLEM 5
Developing Your Own Attitude Scale Items

(1) *Define the attitude*: Define the object of the attitude and the relationship between respondent and object that constitutes the attitude dimension you want to measure.

To be sure you are defining something currently present in social reality, select some object (event, idea, issue, value, person, class, or persons, etc.) about which there is current interest, feeling, or controversy. (Carefully work out a clear but tentative definition.)

(2) *Define the population*: Specify the group, category, type, geographical location, or any other characteristics of the people in whom you expect to find the attitude you have defined.

(3) *Discover relevant items*: Collect some pro and anti statements or questions about the object of the attitude that are meaningful to the population whose attitude is to be measured.

Use sympathetic introspection, participant observation, informal conversation, or unstructured formal interviews with people in the relevant population. How much of these exploratory methods you use will depend upon the amount of time you can spend on the project, the accessibility of the defined population, and whether or not you are a member of that population.

An efficient, minimal exploration can be accomplished if you are a member of the defined population. For example, if each member of a group of students is to design a different attitude scale to be applied to the larger student population, then each member of the group could use sympathetic introspection and memory of his own previous participant observation and informal conversations with fellow students to quickly write some pro and anti statements without concern for the type of content theme, facet-type or potential, answer structure. (A large class could divide into subgroups of four to six people so that each person will have to supply statements on only four to six attitudes.)

(4) *Construct 10 items*: From the raw statements and questions in your pool of "discovered" items first select two which are the most pro and most anti on the basis of their content themes. If there are no extremely pro and extremely anti statements, you should construct at least one of each using the raw materials at hand. After constructing the two extreme items, construct a very mildly pro and a mildly anti item. *Do not try to*

construct a neutral item. (A neutral item has an ambiguous meaning since it does not tell us whether the respondent is against the neutral statement because he is strongly pro or strongly anti. For example, the statement "I feel that blacks and whites are equal" might be viewed as a neutral statement half-way between extreme anti-black and anti-white statements; yet, if the respondent disagrees, there is no way to know whether he or she is pro-black or pro-white.) Now find three positive items to fit in scale order between the strongly anti and the mildly anti items. In constructing the items consider both their content themes and their facet-types in your attempt to place them in predictable scale positions.

ADMINISTERING THE SCALE[5]

Even though great care is taken in designing the written format of the questionnaire, it is possible that in some cases the respondent is not literate enough to cope with it in written form and will have to be interviewed. In this case the interviewer will have to read the statements or questions and the answer categories as well.

Interviewer: "Tell me whether you agree or disagree with this person's statement—let me read it."

"The best thing to do with these militant Indians who want to get all the land back from us where their ancestors used to roam is to give them the choice of the reservation or jail!"

"Would you agree or disagree with that person?"

Respondent: "I'd agree."

Interviewer: "Would you say you agree *strongly* or just agree?"

Respondent: "I really agree strongly with that idea myself."

Obviously, the interview is a much slower process since it involves this much conversation to know that "strongly agree" must be checked for the one item. Furthermore, if interviewing is used, there is no possibility of administering the questionnaire to a group of

---

[5] For a more detailed treatment of the field strategy of administering questionnaires in general see Raymond L. Gorden, *Interviewing: Strategy, Techniques and Tactics* (Homewood, Ill.: Dorsey Press, 1975), particularly the section on Survey Mode, pages 304–309.

people simultaneously or of mailing it to a geographically dispersed sample. Also, it is more difficult to give the respondent the feeling that his response is anonymous since it has to be given orally to the interviewer directly.

If the questionnaire is to be administered to a group of highly literate people, the researcher has an opportunity to induce the proper spontaneous mood in his explanation, but the seating in the group should be such that there is no possibility that any respondent can see how another respondent answers a particular question. In some instances this might be an inhibiting force.

If the questionnaire is to be mailed to isolated individuals in a random sample, the problems of motivation, knowing whether the respondent is literate, and obtaining a complete sample become evident.[6]

[6] *Ibid.*, Chapter 13, "Sample Surveys," pp. 291-329.

Chapter 4. Scalogram Analysis
for Unidimensionality

This discussion of scale analysis assumes that we have (a) defined the attitude to be measured, (b) applied the processes described earlier to discover, select, and construct a set of relevant items, (c) put all of the items into a well-designed questionnaire, (d) identified a sample of the target population, (e) administered the questionnaires, and have the returned questionnaires in hand. We will first review the criteria of scalability or unidimensionality and then show the actual steps in scalogram analysis.

OPERATIONAL CRITERIA OF UNIDIMENSIONALITY

Earlier we pointed out that the Guttman scaling method, unlike most other scaling methods, does not assume that the items researchers feel should make up a scale actually do so. Instead it offers a way of empirically testing the extent to which any set of items constitutes a unidimensional scale at a given moment with a particular population. Furthermore, it provides a measure of unidimensionality known as the *coefficient of reproducibility*. The reproducibility of a particular set of items is the extent to which the total pattern of responses to all items in the set can be "reproduced" precisely and completely from the total score alone. Thus, if a set of items constitutes a unidimensional scale, a single number can represent the whole pattern of responses. In this case each possible total score represents a specific pattern of responses.

This reproducibility can occur only when the relationship between the items is such that they do constitute a unidimensional scale. This means that the items can be arranged in rank order representing their position on a single continuum. The operational evidence of this uni-dimensionality is that the responses to the items placed in rank order demonstrate a *cumulative* relationship. A set of items is cumulative if *persons who answer a given question positively all have higher scores on the scale* (total score) *than persons who answer the same question negatively.*

In order to represent this basic idea graphically, we will assume that we have a scale composed of five items, each having dichotomous answer categories. We will represent a positive answer by (+) and a negative answer by (−). The total score, then, is simply the sum of positive answers in any person's response pattern minus the negative answer.

The cumulative pattern becomes clear only when the response patterns of a number of persons are arranged in a *scalogram* so that (a) the scale items are placed in rank order according to their position on the scale and (b) the respondents are also arranged in rank order according to their total score. In the schematic scalogram in Figure 21 the columns represent the items on the scale and the rows contain the response patterns of each respondent.

Another way of representing the same set of responses to the same items is shown in the dichotomous scalogram in Figure 22. This is a more precise representation of the scalogram technique you will be expected to use in laboratory problems. The scalogram in Figure 22 has the advantages that (a) it will apply to cases where there are more than two possible responses, and (b) the number of response categories can vary from one item to another. The only adjustment

Figure 21. *Schematic Scalogram*

| | Questions or Statements in the Scale | | | | | |
Respondent	Item 1	Item 2	Item 3	Item 4	Item 5	Total score
A	+	+	+	+	+	5
B	+	+	+	+	−	4
C	+	+	+	−	−	3
D	+	+	−	−	−	2
E	+	−	−	−	−	1
F	−	−	−	−	−	0

Respondent	Questions or Statements in the Scale										Total score
	Item 1		Item 2		Item 3		Item 4		Item 5		
	No 0	Yes 1	No 0	Yes 1	No 0	Yes 1	No 0	Yes 1	No 0	Yes 1	
A		x		x		x		x		x	5
B		x		x		x		x	x		4
C		x		x		x	x		x		3
D		x		x	x		x		x		2
E		x	x		x		x		x		1
F	x		x		x		x		x		0

Figure 22. *Dichotomous Scalogram*

needed is to provide the appropriate number of columns under each item to correspond to the number of answer categories in each item. Note that the row (respondent) at which the plus signs changed to minus in the first table is the same point at which the X's move from the "yes" column to the "no" column in the second table.

In either table we can see that the total score corresponds to a particular response pattern:

Total Score		Response Pattern				
5	=	Yes	Yes	Yes	Yes	Yes
4	=	Yes	Yes	Yes	Yes	No
3	=	Yes	Yes	Yes	No	No
2	=	Yes	Yes	No	No	No
1	=	Yes	No	No	No	No
0	=	No	No	No	No	No

The point is that one can predict in advance which questions the person said no to and which he said yes to from the total score alone if the five items belong on the same attitude dimension. Notice that when there are five dichotomous items in the scale, there are six possible total scores. To put this into scaling language, with five dichotomous items in the scale there are six *scale types*. If each item had trichotomous answer categories, there would be 11 possible total scores or scale types.

Logically, there are 32 different combinations of "yes" and "no" answers in groups of five, but only six of these are *scale types*; the remaining 26 are non-scale types. Figure 23 shows the different combinations of answers that could yield each of the total scores ranging from 0 through 5.

Since there are 32 ways of obtaining a score of obtaining a score of from 0 to 5 and only six of these ways are scale types, it is apparent that there is a relatively low probability that a particular person will respond in a scale pattern by pure chance. As the number of items in the scale and the number of answer categories in the set increase, the probability of producing scale types by chance when the items do not belong on a single dimension decreases decidedly.

If a set of items were perfectly scalable and the responses perfectly reliable, then all of the response patterns from any number of respondents would conform to one of the scale types which fits a particular total score. This perfect reproducibility is, of course, never found in reality, but *the coefficient of reproducibility measures the degree of conformity of a set of responses (from a group of respondents) to the perfectly scalable pattern.*

The purpose of the Guttman scaling technique, whether done by hand with a scalogram sheet or by electronic computer, is (a) to determine to what extent the items selected for the scale do or do not constitute a single dimension, and (b) to help purify the scale by eliminating items that do not belong to it and by collapsing answer categories in those items where the group of respondents fail to make the finer distinctions reliably.

Here we will illustrate and explain the steps in measuring the coefficient of reproducibility and purifying the scale in order to increase the reproducibility. As we warned earlier, scaling technique can help with the purification process only if we have been successful initially in including a large portion of items that do in fact belong on a single dimension. We will describe the process of scaling using a scalogram sheet alone without any electronic data processing. Even if a computer were readily available and you were skilled in using it, it would help you to develop more insight and basic understanding to first use the method of the scalogram sheet with small amounts of data and later learn how to feed the data into a computer program.

Figure 23. *Total Scores and Possible Response Patterns*

Total Score	Frequency for answers		Possible Patterns					Total Number of Patterns
	"Yes"	"No"						
5	5	0	+	+	+	+	+	1
4	4	1	+	+	+	+	−	5
			+	+	+	−	+	
			+	+	−	+	+	
			+	−	+	+	+	
			−	+	+	+	+	
3	3	2	+	+	+	−	−	10
			−	+	+	+	−	
			−	−	+	+	+	
			+	+	−	+	−	
			−	+	+	−	+	
			+	−	+	+	−	
			−	+	−	+	+	
			+	−	−	+	+	
			+	+	−	−	+	
			+	−	+	−	+	
2	2	3	+	+	−	−	−	10
			+	−	−	−	+	
			−	−	+	+	+	
			−	−	+	−	+	
			+	−	−	+	−	
			−	+	−	−	+	
			+	−	+	−	−	
			−	+	+	−	−	
			−	−	+	+	−	
			−	+	−	+	−	
1	1	4	+	−	−	−	−	5
			−	+	−	−	−	
			−	−	+	−	−	
			−	−	−	+	−	
			−	−	−	−	+	
0	0	5	−	−	−	−	−	1

Total Number of Patterns   32

STEPS IN SCALOGRAM ANALYSIS

Selecting Cases for Preliminary Scaling

If one is working with a relatively small sample—say, fewer than 50 people—all of the cases could be used for the scalogram test of unidimensionality. But if a sample survey consists of 500 people, it would be unmanageable for scalogram analysis and the analysis would have to use a random sample of the sample survey. For example, we might select every tenth case from the pile of questionnaires and use these 50 cases in the scalogram to test the coefficient of reproducibility.

Editing the Questionnaires

Every questionnaire to be used in the scalogram test should be examined. If certain items were left blank on a questionnaire, it should be eliminated. If it is clear from a totally illogical pattern of responses, from remarks written in, or from any other clues that a particular respondent did not take the task seriously, his or her questionnaire should be eliminated as invalid.

Assigning Scale Values to Answers

The process of assigning scale values to the answers on each questionnaire varies according to which response format was used. You will recall that in using Format A (Figure 18, page 98) it may be necessary to reverse the values of the answer categories for some items if some statements are worded negatively and others positively.

Using one of the blank questionnaires, write an "R" in those blanks where the value of the answer code has to be "reversed" so that the higher number will consistently stand for either the most "pro" or most "anti" feeling. When the response values are totaled, they will then validly indicate the person's position on the scale. By "reversing" the value we mean that a 5 is changed to a 1, a 1 is changed to 5, a 4 is changed to 2, and a 2 to a 4. In a five-point response none of the 3 answers need be changed since this is a neutral category with no direction implied.

The questionnaire on page 98 is an example indicating needed reversals so that a high total score will mean a strong pro attitude.

Please show how much you agree or disagree with each of the statements below, using the following key:

1–Strongly agree
2–Agree
3–Undecided or neutral
4–Disagree
5–Strongly disagree

—— (1) Personally, I hate State College!

—— (2) State College is so bad I have decided to leave at the end of this term.

—— (3) State College is very effective in obstructing real education.

—— (4) State College is a bad scene, but at the moment I am not planning to leave.

—— (5) State College's basic aims are anti-educational, but fortunately it is not very effective in achieving its aims.

—— (6) State College has a lot of shortcomings and nothing will be done about them.

—— (7) My feelings about State College are negative at the moment.

—— (8) State College has some shortcomings that are very unlikely to be corrected.

_R_ (9) If State College has any shortcomings they can be corrected.

_R_(10) State College has a good basic philosophy of education, but it is not carrying it out as effectively as it should.

_R_(11) I have a positive feeling toward State College.

_R_(12) If State College has any shortcomings they will be corrected soon.

_R_(13) State College has an excellent basic educational philosophy and is very effective in carrying it out.

_R_(14) Personally, I love State College.

_R_(15) If some outsider said anything putting down State College I would defend the College.

_R_(16) I am willing to help in the fund-raising drive next week for State College.

In this questionnaire statements regarding attitudes toward State College are arranged in rank order from the most anti in item (1) to the most pro in item (16); items (1) through (8) are negative and items (9) through (16) are positive. Since we said a high total score should indicate a strongly pro attitude, and since in the answer key "strongly agree" has the code number 1, it will be necessary to reverse the code values in all of the positively worded statements so that agreeing strongly with a positive statement will yield a value of 5 on that item instead of 1.

The need for such a reversal key is more obvious in cases where positive and negative statements are intermingled. In this case the reversal key sheet should be trimmed along the left-hand margin so that the answer blanks containing the "R"'s touch the edge. This sheet can be laid on top of each questionnaire so that the two rows of answer spaces are immediately adjacent. Then each answer code number which is beside an "R" item has to be reversed. These reversed numbers can be written in the margin as shown in the cut-out from the same questionnaire.

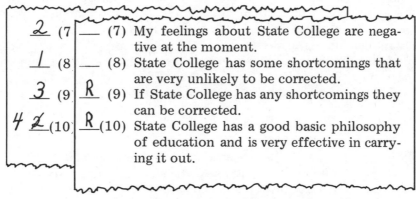

In this example the answer codes given in items (7) and (8) do not need to be reversed since they are negatively worded items. The answer codes for items (9) and (10) are indicated for reversal but in item (9) the answer was a 3, which is not reversible because it is the neutral point on the answer scale of 1 to 5. This leaves only item (10) to be reversed by changing the 2 to a 4.

It is important to cross out the original answer when writing the reversed value in the margin so that there is no danger of adding in the 2 instead of the 4 when arriving at the total score for the questionnaire.

It is possible to key the questionnaire itself to show which items have to be reversed. For example, item numbers for statements worded negatively might use simple parentheses (7) and (8) while numbers for statements worded positively could be underlined, as (9) and (10). The coder can then simply reverse any answer appearing in front of an underlined item number. This system, though more convenient in some ways, tends to increase the error for some coders who would overlook some of the underlinings.

If Formats B or C are used, there is no need to make any reversals in assigning the scale values to each response. If you use Format C (Figure 20) it is advisable to write the appropriate scale value in the margin just in front of the item number. In this case, as mentioned earlier, every answer checked on the extreme left has a value of 5 and the others are valued accordingly.

Calculating the Total Scores

Once all the scale values have been written in for all items on all the questionnaires, the values of all the items are added to obtain a total score. The total score should be written in large, clear, and unambiguous writing in the upper right-hand corner of each questionnaire. If there is more than one page to the questionnaire, put the total score on the front page. To avoid errors it is advisable to use an adding machine even though you are summing only a few single-digit numbers. Errors in addition will put the person in the wrong rank order in the scalogram.

Arranging Questionnaires in Rank Order

Simply arrange all the questionnaires in a pile in rank order, with the highest total score on the top. If there are ties in scores, keep those questionnaires together.

Recording the Responses on the Scalogram Sheet

Make a scalogram sheet on which to record the responses by adapting the sample sheet shown in Figure 24. This scalogram is designed to handle up to 30 respondents to a questionnaire with up to 10 items, each having as many as five answer categories. If there are more than 30 respondents, simply extend the scalogram by gluing on a second sheet at the bottom edge. If there are more than 10 items in the questionnaire, extend the right side of the sheet in the same manner. If there are more than five answer categories for some items, renumber the columns to accommodate all the answer categories for each item.

Once your scalogram sheet is ready, take the questionnaire with the highest total score and record all the responses on the first row of the sheet. First write the total score in the "score" column. Then put an "X" in the appropriate cell under each item number. On the scalo-

Figure 24. Blank Scalogram

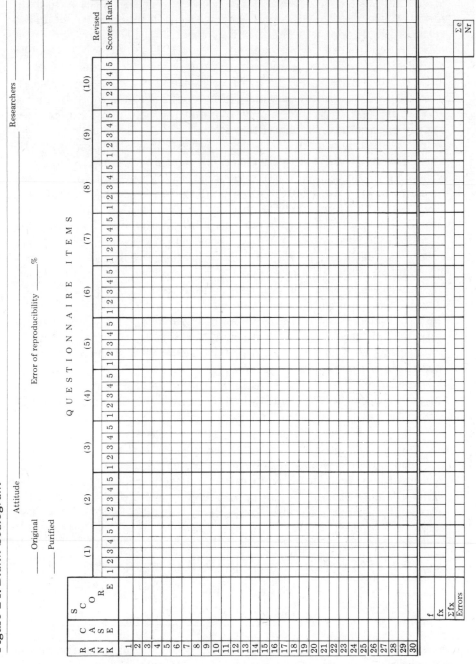

gram sheet the numbers 1 to 5 under each item number represent the scale values of the response after the necessary reversals have been made. These are the same numbers you have just summed to obtain the total score. Proceed in this fashion, recording all the responses on each questionnaire in rank order of total score. Check as you go along to be sure the total scores appear in descending order.

Once all the responses have been recorded on the scalogram sheet, you are ready to begin calculating the coefficient of reproducibility and trying to purify the scale by eliminating some items and collapsing the answer categories on other items.

The appearance of the pattern of real data in a scalogram might be quite different from the idealized illustration of scalability given earlier in Figure 22. It was a very small scalogram that for the sake of simplicity showed only six respondents to a questionnaire of only five items. Furthermore, for the sake of conceptual clarity we assumed that the responses were all dichotomous and that the items were arranged in order according to their position on the scale. However, in actual practice we may try to arrange the items on the questionnaire in what we expect to be their scale order but fail to do so. The correct order can be determined after the data are collected by calculating the mean scale value of the group's responses to each item. It is necessary to have the items in rank order in the scalogram only to illustrate clearly the idea of scalable response patterns. In actual practice it is possible to test the scalability of the set of items regardless of their order in the scalogram.

Because of these differences between the ideal scalogram for illustrative purposes and the real scalogram in practice, the real one might appear to have a pattern of responses that appears at first glance to be totally chaotic. This does not mean that the set of items is not scalable. To obtain a better understanding of how real responses are arranged into a scalogram, you should try to construct the scalogram in Laboratory Problem 6 from questionnaire responses that are perfectly scalable. Later in Laboratory Problem 7 you can work with response patterns that are not perfectly scalable and measure the "error of reproducibility" which is the amount of deviation from perfect scalability.

LABORATORY PROBLEM 6
Constructing a Scalogram

This problem focuses on the operations necessary to organize a sample of responses into the form of a scalogram. Three major steps are involved: (a) studying the questionnaire (page 104) to determine which items need to have the answer code numbers reversed in order to become scale values, (b) analyzing the data summary sheet to determine the rank order of both the respondents and the questions, and (c) transferring the values from the data summary sheet to the scalogram sheet while rearranging the order of both the respondents and the questions.

A. *Study the Questionnaire (see the next page).* The questionnaire used at State U. was refined from the previous one used at State College, and was designed to measure the amount of fear of physical violence on a university campus during the upheavals of the early 1970s. Study the relationships of the 10 items to one another and do operations (1) and (2).

 (1) *Translate answer-code numbers to scale values.* The respondents are asked to use the answer codes 1 through 5 to designate the amount of agreement or disagreement. But since some of the items are worded in a pro-violence direction and others are reversed, it is necessary to reverse the code values on some items by changing the 5 code to 1, the 4 to 2, and vice versa, leaving all the 3 codes unchanged. In which two of the ten items should the answer codes be reversed to convert into scale values?

 (2) *Predict the rank order of items on the scale.* Compare the 10 statements to predict which represents the greatest and the least fear of campus violence. Put them in rank order, with number 1 for the most violence, on an answer sheet as follows.

Questionnaire item	1	2	3	4	5	6	7	8	9	10
Scale order										

 After you have analyzed the data summary sheet you will be able to verify your prediction of rank order.

B. *Analyze the Data Summary Sheet.* As an alternative to giving you 20 questionnaires filled out by the sample of respondents, we have presented the data in the more compact form of the data summary sheet in Figure 25. The names of the 20 respondents are arranged in alphabetical order. The columns are numbered from 1 to 10 corresponding to the item numbers on the questionnaire you have just studied. The numbers in the cells are the response code numbers that were written on the questionnaires.

 There is no way of verifying whether these 10 items consti-

Questionnaire   —— Female
                                 —— Male

Below are ten statements about possible physical violence at State U. Indicate how much you agree or disagree with each using the following key:

> 1-Strongly agree
> 2-Agree
> 3-Undecided
> 4-Disagree
> 5-Strongly disagree

—— (1) "The danger of violence at State has become so great that I have decided to transfer to another college."

—— (2) State U. is the safest place anyone could possibly find to live."

—— (3) "I'm afraid of the possibility of physical assault most of the time I am on the campus."

—— (4) "Although there is occasional violence, State U. is much safer than other colleges in the country."

—— (5) "Many people at State U. are worried about possible violence on Campus."

—— (6) "I am often uneasy about possible violence at State U."

—— (7) "Many people at State U. avoid certain situations because they are afraid of possible physical assault."

—— (8) "Any realistic and intelligent person is anxious about possible physical assault at State U."

—— (9) "I never walk across campus alone at night for fear of possible assault."

——(10) "It is not generally safe to walk around campus at night alone."

Respondents (N = 20)	Items in Questionnaire Order										Total Score	Rank
	1	2	3	4	5	6	7	8	9	10		
Anne	4	5	2	5	2	1	1	1	1	1		
Betty	5	5	5	5	5	3	5	2	4	3		
Charlotte	5	5	5	5	4	1	3	1	3	1		
Donald	4	5	3	5	3	1	2	1	1	1		
Elwood	5	5	4	5	4	1	3	1	2	1		
Frieda	4	5	2	5	1	1	1	1	1	1		
Greg	5	5	3	5	4	1	2	1	1	1		
Harry	5	5	5	5	5	3	5	2	5	3		
Irene	5	5	5	4	5	4	5	3	5	5		
James	4	5	3	5	2	1	1	1	1	1		
Karen	5	5	5	5	4	1	3	1	2	1		
Lorraine	5	5	5	5	5	2	5	1	4	2		
Marty	5	4	5	3	5	4	5	4	5	5		
Nancy	5	5	4	5	4	1	2	1	1	1		
Oliver	5	5	5	5	5	1	4	1	4	1		
Peter	5	5	3	5	3	1	2	1	1	1		
Quincy	4	5	3	5	3	1	1	1	1	1		
Ray	5	5	4	5	4	1	2	1	2	1		
Steve	5	3	5	3	5	5	5	4	5	5		
Tom	5	5	5	4	5	3	5	3	5	4		
Total Value											528	
Rank												

Figure 25. *Data Summary Sheet*

tute a unidimensional scale for the sample of 20 respondents as long as the data are in this raw summary form. To make the scalability *visible* we must rearrange the rows (respondents) and columns (items) so that both are in rank order according to their total values. To determine the appropriate rank order for items and respondents, perform operations (3) through (8) below.

(3) *Translate code numbers to scale values.* In the two columns representing items you designated for reversal (step 1), write in the reversed values as you go down the column.

(4) *Obtain total scale value for each item.* Add up all of the numbers in each column (be sure you use the scale values instead of the original code numbers in those columns where numbers were reversed) and enter the figure in the "Total Value" row at the bottom.

(5) *Obtain total score for each person.* Add up each row, again watching for the translated values, and put the sum in the "Total Score" column at the right.

(6) *Check row and column totals.* Add all the row totals to obtain a grand total. Then add all the column totals to see if the same grand total results. If not, you have made an error in adding at some point. (The grand total should be 528.)

(7) *Rank the items.* Rank the items (columns) according to the total scale value of the responses to the items, using 1 for the largest total value. Thus item 1 with a total value of 95 is rank one while item 2 with the smallest total value of 23 is rank ten. Write in the ranks from 1 to 10 in the "Rank" row at the bottom.

(8) *Rank the respondents.* Rank the respondents' total scores using 1 for the largest score. Thus, Steve, who has a score of 45, is given rank 1, and Frieda, who has a score of 14, is given rank 20.

C. *Transfer data to the Scalogram.* The most exacting operation is converting the information on the data summary sheet into the scalogram. Use a blank scalogram sheet (Figure 24) and do the work in pencil so that errors can be corrected.

(9) *Reorder the respondents.* Fill in each respondent's initial in the "case" column on the scalogram (Figure 26) in the *rank order* indicated in the "rank" column on the data summary sheet. If you have done this correctly the initials reading down the column should spell the name of three undistinguished people by the name of Smith, Blockering, and P. D. Q. Jaf.)

(10) *Transfer the data by rank order of items.* Transfer the information from the data summary sheet to the scalogram, starting with the row for Steve's responses (row 19 in the data summary sheet). Enter his scale values in row 1 of the scalogram. Enter the value for each item according to the *rank order* of the total scale value as indicated in the bottom row of the data summary sheet. Put an "X" in the appropriate column to indicate the scale value from 1 to 5.

Note that there are two designations in the scalogram for each of the ten items. The uppermost set of numbers 1 to 10 refers to the original number of the item in the questionnaire and summary sheet. They have been arranged in order to correspond to the rank order of their position on the scale as indicated by the second level of numbers in parentheses.

Figure 26. Short Scalogram Form

Name _____

QUESTIONNAIRE ITEMS

R A N K	C A S E	Item	Rank	Score	*1* (1)	*3* (2)	*5* (3)	*7* (4)	*9* (5)	*10* (6)	*6* (7)	*8* (8)	*4* (9)	*2* (10)
1	S		5	45	X (5)	X (5)	X (5)	X (5)	X (5)	X (5)	X (5)	X (5)	X (5)	X (3)
2														
3														
4														
5														
6														
7														
8														
9														
10														
11														
12														
13														
14														
15														
16														
17														
18														
19														
20	F		14		X (1)	X (1)	X (1)	X (1)	X (1)	X (1)	X (1)	X (1)	X (1)	X (1)

Be sure to enter the responses in the correct order of the items. The responses have already been recorded in the first and last rows of the scalogram to illustrate the process. Check this carefully and do the same for the remaining 18 cases.

Discussion

If you have completed these processes successfully you should have a scalogram with zero error of reproducibility. This is demonstrated if for each item the pattern of responses always progresses from right to left as we scan down the column. This is the visual manifestation of the principle that a set of items constitutes a cumulative scale if persons who answer a given question more favorably all have higher total scores than persons who answer the same question less favorably. Another visual manifestation of scalability occurs when the items are arranged in rank order according to their total scale value and the progression of X's from any given scale-value column to the next lower-valued column always occurs first in the item at the extreme right, then in the next item in rank order, and so on toward the left.

In this case there is no need to calculate the error reproducibility because there are no deviations from the pattern of perfect scalability defined above. This first empirical case may appear to have a less regular pattern than is presented in the previous hypothetical examples. This is because the small sample of 20 cases does not include all the possible scores of the range between 10 and 50. You may have noted that the scores often skip two or three points in the upper portion of the range, from 45 down to 25.

In the next laboratory problem you will have an opportunity to measure the amount of deviation from the perfectly scalable pattern.

CALCULATING THE COEFFICIENT OF REPRODUCIBILITY

In commonsense terms, the coefficient of reproducibility can be defined as the extent to which the total response pattern on a questionnaire can be reproduced if only the total score is known. Mathematically the coefficient is the percentage of the total responses from any sample of respondents which can be reproduced on the basis of the individuals' total scores only. This of course depends upon the extent to which the pattern of responses for the whole sample of respondents conforms to a perfectly scalable pattern. In order to understand the meaning of the term "perfectly scalable pattern" it is helpful to inspect a number of scalogram sheets with the perfectly scalable response patterns filled in and to compare these with scalograms containing real response patterns in some systematic way. Never do the real responses conform 100% to the perfect pattern.

In most explanations of Guttman scaling, items with dichotomous answer categories are used to illustrate the perfect scale; then the reader is advised to use three, four, or five answer categories in practice. We have found that this hiatus between theory and practice is often a source of confusion and error when a researcher tries to calculate the coefficient of reproducibility. We therefore will illustrate the idea of a perfect scale using items with five answer categories from the beginning.

The confusion arises when we discover that only in the special case of dichotomous answer categories is it true that there is one and only one way to obtain a particular total score if the responses follow a scalable pattern. Here we will not consider the mathematical problem of how to determine the number of different scale types (total pattern of responses of one person to all of the items) possible with a given number of items and response categories. But we will illustrate the fact that when three or more answer categories are used, there is more than one possible pattern of perfectly scalable responses. To state this in another way, there will be more than one pattern of answers which will total up to the same score.

Before we can illustrate this, however, it is necessary to establish our definition of "perfectly scalable pattern." To do this let me quote Guttman and then paraphrase in more concrete language directly applicable to responses to a questionnaire.

> There is unambiguous meaning to the order of scale scores and the order of categories within each item. An object with a higher score than another object is characterized by higher, or at least equivalent, values on every attribute. Similarly, one category of an item is higher than another if it characterizes persons all of whom are higher on the scale.[1]

> A set of responses to a questionnaire item can be considered scalable if there is an unambiguous meaning to the total scores. This is the case when a person with a higher total score than another person is characterized by higher, or at least equivalent, values of his responses to each and every item in the questionnaire. Similarly, one answer category can be said to have a higher value

[1] Louis L. Guttman, "The Basis for Scalogram Analysis," Chapter 13 in G. M. Maranell (ed.), *Scaling: A Sourcebook for Behavioral Scientists* (Chicago: Aldine Publishing Co., 1974), pp. 142–71.

than another answer category for that same item on the questionnaire if it characterizes persons all of whom have a higher total score.

Now if we carefully inspect scalogram patterns A, B, and C in Figures 27, 28, and 29, respectively, we see that the three patterns are distinctly different, yet all three fulfill the criteria of a scalable pattern of responses. These three are not the only perfect scale patterns that can be obtained with a set of items having five response categories each, but they are sufficient to illustrate many important considerations that arise in practice.

First, note that all three patterns are alike in several ways: (a) there are 25 respondents represented by the 25 rows; (b) there are six items with five answer categories each, represented by the 30 columns in six groups of five columns each; (c) the respondents are arranged in rank order according to their total scores; (d) these total scores range from the maximum possible (30 on this scale) to the minimum possible (6), giving a 25-point range of scores; (e) in each case the items are arranged in order of their position on the scale; and (f) each pattern is such that it fulfills the criteria of a scalable pattern of responses.

Second, note that there are important differences among the three scalogram patterns. For example, patterns A and B represent extreme types with C falling in between. In the case of pattern A, as we move downward from the highest score of 30, we note that there is no change in the pattern of responses on items 1, 2, 3, 4, and 5 until the responses have moved through the full range (5, 4, 3, 2, 1) on item 6. Of course as we move further downward in the pattern, all of the remaining respondents must give a 1 response to item 6 in order to fulfill one basic criterion of the scalable pattern. Then, in turn, as we move downward, there is no change in the pattern of responses on items 1, 2, 3, and 4 until the responses have moved through the full range (5, 4, 3, 2, 1) on item 5. Then as we proceed further downward in the pattern, all of the remaining respondents give a 1 response to item 5, conforming to the scalable pattern. This pattern is followed through item 4, item 3, item 2, and finally item 1 until the lowest possible total score of 6 is reached. Pattern A is perfectly scalable.

Now look at pattern B. This pattern, which is visibly different, also fulfills the criteria of a perfect pattern, but it seems to follow a different formula. Here the rule is the opposite of that followed in pattern A. Instead of first exhausting the full range of response pattern to item 6, then using the full range of item 5, and so on, this scalogram seems to follow the rule that item 6 should first move one point in its range and then hold at that position until each of the remaining five items in turn (5, 4, 3, 2, 1) has used only one point in

Figure 27. Perfect Reproducibility Pattern A

RANK	Scores
1	30
2	29
3	28
4	27
5	26
6	25
7	24
8	23
9	22
10	21
11	20
12	19
13	18
14	17
15	16
16	15
17	14
18	13
19	12
20	11
21	10
22	9
23	8
24	7
25	6

(1) (2) (3) (4) (5) (6)

f
fx
Σx

(a.)
(b.)
(c.)
(d.) Item Distance

Figure 28. *Perfect Reproducibility Pattern B*

RANK	Scores	(1)					(2)					(3)					(4)					(5)					(6)				
		1	2	3	4	5	1	2	3	4	5	1	2	3	4	5	1	2	3	4	5	1	2	3	4	5	1	2	3	4	5
1	30					X					X					X					X					X					X
2	29					X					X					X					X					X				X	
3	28					X					X					X					X				X					X	
4	27					X					X					X				X					X					X	
5	26					X					X				X					X					X					X	
6	25					X				X					X					X					X					X	
7	24				X					X					X					X					X					X	
8	23				X					X					X					X					X				X		
9	22				X					X					X					X				X					X		
10	21				X					X					X				X					X					X		
11	20				X					X				X					X					X					X		
12	19				X				X					X					X					X					X		
13	18			X					X					X					X					X					X		
14	17			X					X					X					X					X				X			
15	16			X					X					X					X				X					X			
16	15			X					X					X				X					X					X			
17	14			X					X				X					X					X					X			
18	13			X				X					X					X					X					X			
19	12		X					X					X					X					X					X			
20	11		X					X					X					X					X				X				
21	10		X					X					X					X				X					X				
22	9		X					X					X				X					X					X				
23	8		X					X				X					X					X					X				
24	7		X				X					X					X					X					X				
25	6	X					X					X					X					X					X				
(a)	f	1	6	6	6	6	2	6	6	6	5	3	6	6	6	4	4	6	6	6	3	5	6	6	6	2	6	6	6	6	1
(b.)	fx	1	12	18	24	30	2	12	18	24	25	3	12	18	24	20	4	12	18	24	15	5	12	18	24	10	6	12	18	24	5
(C.)	Σx	85					81					77					73					69					65				
(d)	Item Distance					4					4					4					4					4					

Figure 29. *Perfect Reproducibility Pattern C*

		(1)					(2)					(3)					(4)					(5)					(6)				
RANK	Scores	1	2	3	4	5	1	2	3	4	5	1	2	3	4	5	1	2	3	4	5	1	2	3	4	5	1	2	3	4	5
1	30					X					X					X					X					X					X
2	29					X					X					X					X					X				X	
3	28					X					X					X					X				X					X	
4	27					X					X					X				X					X					X	
5	26					X					X					X				X					X				X		
6	25					X					X					X				X				X					X		
7	24					X					X					X			X					X					X		
8	23					X					X					X			X					X				X			
9	22					X					X					X			X				X					X			
10	21					X					X					X		X					X					X			
11	20					X					X					X		X					X				X				
12	19					X					X					X		X				X					X				
13	18					X					X					X	X					X					X				
14	17					X					X				X		X					X					X				
15	16					X				X					X		X					X					X				
16	15				X					X					X		X					X					X				
17	14				X					X				X			X					X					X				
18	13				X				X					X			X					X					X				
19	12			X					X					X			X					X					X				
20	11			X					X				X				X					X					X				
21	10			X				X					X				X					X					X				
22	9		X					X					X				X					X					X				
23	8		X					X				X					X					X					X				
24	7		X				X					X					X					X					X				
25	6	X					X					X					X					X					X				
(a.)	f	1	3	3	3	15	2	3	3	3	14	3	3	3	3	13	13	3	3	3	3	14	3	3	3	2	15	3	3	3	1
(b.)	fx	1	6	9	12	75	2	6	9	12	70	3	6	9	12	65	13	6	9	12	15	14	6	9	12	10	15	6	9	12	5
(c.)	Σx	103					99					95					55					51					47				
(d.)	Item Distance					4					4					40					4					4					

its range. Although pattern B is entirely different from pattern A, it nevertheless fulfills the criteria of a perfectly scalable pattern.

Similarly, pattern C fulfills the criteria of a perfect pattern but seems to be somewhere between patterns A and B in that item 6 neither runs through its full range of responses before item 5 as in pattern A, nor does it wait until all five of the other items on the scale respond before it responds again as is the case in pattern B. Instead, it seems to follow the rule that after it has responded with one degree change it holds that position until two other items have responded in turn. This rule produces patterns of three responses in the same category as we move downward in the pattern.

Empirically, I have discovered that some sets of questions with five response categories tend to produce a pattern of responses that more closely resembles pattern A and some are more like B, some more like C, and others seem to be mixed. Although I have not seen a mathematical explanation of how or why these different patterns appear, I will venture a suggestion on the basis of intuitive inspection of the relationship between the pattern of responses and the kind of questions used. Pattern A seems to result when the questions are such that they are spaced further apart on the attitude dimension; pattern B seems to result when the items are psychologically closer together or even overlapping in their range.

This hypothesis is consistent with the analysis of these three patterns. If you look at rows (a), (b), (c), and (d) at the bottom of each scalogram, you will see that row (a) gives the number of responses to each category of an item. Each group of five responses always gives a total of 25 since there were 25 respondents in this sample. Row (b) is a value obtained by multiplying the number of responses in row (a) by the scale value of that response, shown at the top of the column. Row (c) is the sum of the five values for each item on the questionnaire. If the items on the questionnaire have been arranged in order according to their position on the attitude scale, then the total values in row (c) will proceed continuously through either an ascending or a descending order, as shown in all three of the scalograms.

The striking difference among the three scalograms shows in a comparison of rows (c) and (d). The differences between the row (c) values for adjacent items called the *item distance*, is given in row (d). Note that the distance between items in scalogram A is uniform (16 points) and that the distance between items in scalogram B is also uniform but much smaller (4 points). When we inspect the item distance for scalogram C, we note that it is uniform at each end of the scale, but that a large gap (40 points) is found between items 3 and 4 in the middle of the scale.

The crucial point here is that there are different possible perfect-scale patterns when there are more than two answer categories; the same total score will represent different scale patterns. We can see by comparing the tables that only four of the possible total scores (between 6 and 30) have only one possible response pattern as a scale type. These are scores 6, 7, 29, 30. Thus, the two scores at each extreme of the scale have the same pattern of responses in all three scalograms. But if we compare the three scalograms for the patterns corresponding to the scores of 8 and 9 at the lower end, or 27 and 28 at the upper end, we note that there are two different patterns. We can see that as we move toward the center of the scale range all three of the scalograms have a different pattern for the same score.

Under these conditions, introduced by using more than two answer categories with each item, it is possible to obtain 100% reproducibility in a sample of respondents only if all persons in the sample having the same total score are following the same scalable pattern of responses. In the three perfect scalogram patterns given here, there is only one respondent representing each of the possible scores from 6 through 30. If we had a sample of 100 respondents, there would be an average of four persons having each score since there are only 25 possible total scores. Whether or not the items would be scalable for a particular sample of respondents would depend on (in addition to other things) whether all those people having the same score had the same response pattern.

Figure 30 illustrates three patterns of perfect conformity, each of which would yield a coefficient of reproducibility of 100%, and a fourth pattern which is a mixture of the other three patterns and has a much lower coefficient of reproducibility.

Each of these four examples covers only three of the scores (26, 27, and 28) in the upper portion of the full range, so the differences among the patterns are manifested only in items on one end of the scale (items 3, 4, 5, 6); no differences appear in the patterns for items 1 and 2. If we had compared the lower end of the range of total scores there would also be differences in the patterns for items 1 and 2.

Patterns A, B, and C in Figure 30 correspond to patterns A, B, and C in Figures 27, 28, and 29. The "mixed pattern" at the bottom of Figure 30 contains all three patterns, as indicated by the letters after each score. The difference in appearance between the patterns in Figure 30 and those in Figures 27, 28, and 29 is due to the fact that there are tie scores in the patterns in Figure 30.

Note that in each of the first three patterns there is no error of reproducibility because in the case of tie scores the respondents all followed the same scale pattern. Therefore, the pattern of responses for any given item, as we proceed downward, always moves to the left and never moves back again. However, in the mixed example,

Pattern A

Scores	(1)					(2)					(3)					(4)					(5)					(6)				
	1	2	3	4	5	1	2	3	4	5	1	2	3	4	5	1	2	3	4	5	1	2	3	4	5	1	2	3	4	5
28				X						X					X					X				X			X			
28				X						X				X						X				X				X		
27				X						X					X					X					X	X				
27				X						X					X					X				X		X				
27				X						X					X				X					X		X				
26				X						X					X				X					X		X				

Pattern B

Scores	(1)					(2)					(3)					(4)					(5)					(6)				
	1	2	3	4	5	1	2	3	4	5	1	2	3	4	5	1	2	3	4	5	1	2	3	4	5	1	2	3	4	5
28				X						X					X				X					X						X
28				X						X					X				X					X						X
27				X						X					X			X						X						X
27				X						X					X			X						X						X
27				X						X					X			X						X						X
26				X						X			X					X						X						X

Pattern C

Scores	(1)					(2)					(3)					(4)					(5)					(6)				
	1	2	3	4	5	1	2	3	4	5	1	2	3	4	5	1	2	3	4	5	1	2	3	4	5	1	2	3	4	5
28				X						X					X				X				X							X
28				X						X					X				X				X							X
27				X						X					X			X					X							X
27				X						X					X			X					X							X
27				X						X					X			X					X							X
26				X						X					X			X					X						X	

Mixed Pattern

Scores	(1)					(2)					(3)					(4)					(5)					(6)				
	1	2	3	4	5	1	2	3	4	5	1	2	3	4	5	1	2	3	4	5	1	2	3	4	5	1	2	3	4	5
28A				X						X				X					X					X		⊗				
28B				X						X				X					X		⊗									X
27A				X						X				X					X						X	⊗				
27B				X						X				X				X						X						X
27CC				X						X				X				X						X						X
26C				X						X				X				X						X				X		

Figure 30. *Alternative and Mixed Scalable Patterns*

the response on item (6) moves right, then left, then right, then left again. The meaning of the total score, 28, is ambiguous because there are two different patterns of response receiving that same score. Thus, the total pattern of response is not reliably reproducible from the total score. This situation is called *error of reproducibility* and is expressed as the percentage of the responses that deviate from a scalable pattern.

In the mixed example, the three responses that are circled are considered errors since they deviate from the pattern. They violate the rule of a steady unidirectional progression from right to left as we proceed from higher total scores to lower scores. Since there are 36 responses (six respondents times six items) and only three errors, there are 33 non-errors out of 36 responses. The coefficient of reproducibility is 33/36, or 91.6%, in this case. In a sociogram containing more respondents, more items, and more errors, it is not so easy to distinguish errors from the non-errors. To do this we must understand the concept of *cutting points*.

Choosing Cutting Points

A cutting point is that point in the column of responses to a single questionnaire item in the scalogram where the pattern would shift from one response category (column) to another if the item were perfectly scalable. If a particular item has a perfect pattern, progressing in an orderly fashion from column to column as it proceeds downward, without ever reversing direction, then there is no problem in seeing the cutting point. For example, in item A of Figure 31, the response pattern is perfect, and the point at which the pattern shifts response categories is clear and unambiguous.

In item B the one circled response deviates from the steady progression of the perfect pattern, yet there is little difficulty in seeing the underlying pattern. In item C there is more deviation from the perfect pattern, and locating the cutting point is more problematical. The cutting points chosen result in the two circled errors, but there are other possibilities. For example, if the researcher had decided that the "true" scalable pattern was such that all eight of the responses at the top of the pattern really belonged in category 3, the first cutting point would be eliminated, resulting in three errors as shown in CC. Since the cutting points established as in item C result in fewer errors than in item CC, which has precisely the same response pattern, it is clear that the cutting point in C is correct since it minimizes the error.

In some cases, as in item D, the pattern is such that no matter where the cutting point is located there will be considerable error. For example, if we assume that the first nine responses really belong in category 4, then we would have to consider the four responses in category 3 as "errors." If, on the other hand, we assume that all nine responses belong in category 3, then the five responses in category 4 become the "errors." The amount of error could be reduced to three by establishing a cutting point at the dotted line shown.

Figure 31. *Cutting Points*

Rank	Score	A 1 2 3 4 5	B 1 2 3 4 5	C 1 2 3 4 5	CC 1 2 3 4 5	D 1 2 3 4 5
1						
2						
3						
4						
5						
6						
7						
8						
9						
10						
11						
12						
13						
14						
15						
16						
17						
18						
19						
20						

There are also cases where the vacillation of responses between two adjacent categories is such that one cutting point is no better than another. In these cases the solution may be to collapse the two adjacent categories into one. This process will be explained later.

Calculating the Error of Reproducibility

Now that the cutting points have been established and the deviant responses circled, we can calculate the percentage error of reproducibility. In Figure 31, since there are 20 respondents and four items (after omitting CC, which is a duplication of C), we know that there are 80 responses. The total number of errors in the four items is 7; therefore the error of reproducibility is 7/80, or 8.75%.

Converting to the Coefficient of Reproducibility

The coefficient of reproducibility is simply the amount of "non-error" in the scalogram. Since the number of errors plus the number of non-errors in the scalogram equals the total number of responses in the scalogram, we know that if there is 8.75% error, there is 91.25% non-error; therefore, the coefficient of reproducibility is 91.25%. According to Guttman, a coefficient of reproducibility of 90% is high enough to indicate that the set of items constitutes a unidimensional scale if certain additional criteria are also met.

Laboratory Problem 7 provides practice in calculating the error of reproducibility.

LABORATORY PROBLEM 7
Calculating the Error of Reproducibility

In Laboratory Problem 6 you constructed a scalogram that showed the data to be perfectly scalable. This rarely occurs in reality. There is nearly always some deviation from the perfect scale pattern, particularly when five answer categories are used rather than the simple dichotomous form. Figure 32 is a scalogram of the responses to 10 items by a real sample of 30 people. Your task is to take all the necessary steps to calculate the error of reproducibility.

The respondents have been arranged in the rows of the scalogram according to the rank order of their total scores. These scores range from 20 to 47; the maximum possible range is 10 to 50. The items have been arranged according to the scale order *expected* by the person constructing the scale. Study the whole pattern of the scalogram and make a guess as to what the percent error of reproduci-

Figure 32. Scalogram Data for Laboratory Problem 7

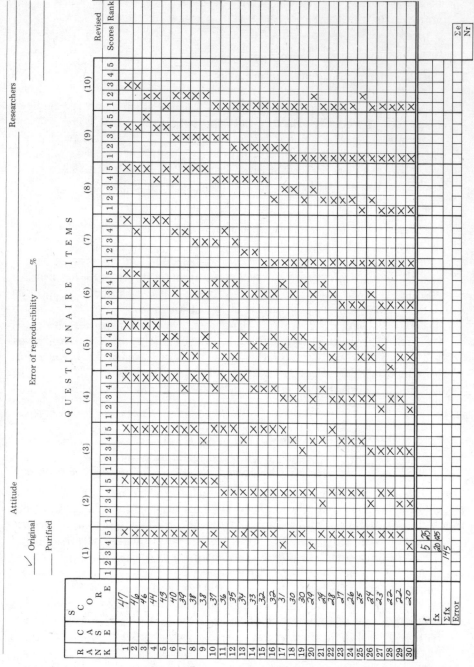

bility will be. Write this figure in the blank provided on your answer sheet.

(1) *Calculate the real scale position of the items.* In the "f" row at the bottom of the scalogram, write in the total number of responses in each column. Check to see that the frequencies in the five columns for each item add up to 30. Now multiply each number in the "f" row by the scale value of that column and write the product in the "fx" row just below. Then add the fx values in the five columns for each item and put that sum in the Σfx row. These numbers show the rank position of the item on the scale. This calculation is illustrated for item number 1 only. Do this for the remaining nine items and then write the new *rank order* of the Σfx in the blanks provided on your answer sheet.

Was the researcher who constructed the items correct in predicting the scale order of the 10 items?

Although it is absolutely necessary to arrange the respondents (rows) in rank order on the scalogram, it is not necessary to arrange the items in their scale position in order to count the errors and calculate the error of reproducibility. As has been shown in Figure 31 errors are demonstrated in the scalogram display as deviations from the perfectly scalable pattern within each item independently, therefor the total error can be obtained by adding the errors in the separate items. This is why the order of the items in the scalogram is not essential to testing the scalability of the items.

(2) *Establish cutting points.* Look at the pattern of responses to each item and put in the cutting points so as to minimize the number of errors. *Do this in pencil* so that errors may be corrected.

(3) *Count the number of errors.* Circle each response that does not conform to the scalable pattern. Count the number of these errors in each column and write the figure in the row for "errors" at the bottom of the scalogram. Then add all of the errors for all 10 items and put the sum in the cell labeled Σe at the right end of the bottom row.

(4) *Calculate the error of reproducibility.* Divide the Σe by the total number of responses in the scalogram (30 respondents times 10 items equals 300 responses) and multiply by 100 to obtain the percent error of reproducibility. Write this figure in the blank provided at the top of the scalogram.

Did you anticipate this error of reproducibility when you first looked at the scalogram? Why? Why not?

(In the next Laboratory Problem you will use the same set of scalogram data and "purify" the scale either by rejecting items that don't seem to belong or by combining answer categories where the scalogram suggests that the distinctions between certain adjacent answer categories are unreliable.)

Chapter 5.   Purifying the Scale

If we find that the coefficient of reproducibility is below 90%, we can attempt to increase the coefficient by either (a) rejecting those items that contribute outstandingly to the total error of reproducibility or (b) collapsing two or more adjacent response categories into one in items where the response pattern vacillates among those categories. Whichever form of purification is attempted, there is a low probability of improving the coefficient of reproducibility unless most of the items actually belong on a single dimension.

Removing one item from the scale or collapsing answer categories in an item does not necessarily reduce the total number of errors by the number the rejected or corrected items had contributed. This is true because after the attempted purification we must *rescore* each respondent's questionnaire with the rejected items omitted and with the new values assigned to the collapsed categories. When all the respondents have been assigned new scores there will usually be some change in the rank order of the scores. When the new scalogram is constructed with the respondents in a slightly different rank order, it is probable that some of the responses which were not errors on the first scalogram will become errors on the second scalogram.

To a great extent this purification process is a trial-and-error method; the attempts to raise the coefficient of reproducibility may succeed or fail. If the apparent scalability of the first scalogram was largely spurious or accidental, then it is possible that the attempt at purification will *increase* the error of reproducibility or make no change. In my experience, if the initial coefficient of reproducibility is below 80%, it is often impossible to raise it to 90%, but if the initial scale has 85% reproducibility, it is not unusual to be able to raise it to 95% through the purification process.

Even though there is a strong element of trial and error in the purification process, success does depend to some extent on having good criteria for rejecting items or collapsing categories, and some experience and insight into the application of these criteria. Let us now examine some of these criteria.

REJECTING OFFENDING ITEMS

When we have a scalogram with the errors circled, we must be guided by some clear criteria to decide which errors to try to correct. It is logically and mathematically impossible to eliminate all of the errors. We must be selective; otherwise, the attempt at purification may increase the amount of error. There are three major criteria which should be used in deciding which items to eliminate: the patterns of error within a single item, the position of the item in the range of the scale, and the amount of error in the response pattern to the item. Let us examine each of these criteria in turn.

Patterns of Error

Edward A. Suchman[1] points out that there are patterns of error just as there are patterns of scalability. Even though three items may have precisely equal *amounts* of error, the *patterns* may be meaningfully different. For example, in Figure 33 the three items (A, B, and C) each have 20% error (10 out of 50), but they represent three basically different patterns.

Item A has a pattern of responses that Suchman calls *random scale errors*. There are five errors distributed randomly above the cutting point and another five errors distributed randomly below the cutting point. (Here we have used items with dichotomous answer categories to simplify the exposition.) Such an item is *not* a candidate for rejection because this random error is likely to appear in the best of items and may have nothing to do with whether or not the item belongs in a set comprising a scale. Instead, it might represent error due to a random lack of reliability because of inattentiveness of respondents to some items, or to the random probability that certain respondents are generally misinterpreting the instructions or have some personality characteristic operating in addition to their attitude measured by the scale. Also, there may be other attitude dimensions entering the area in the minds of some respondents. Whatever the

[1] Edward A. Suchman, "The Utility of Scalogram Analysis," Chapter 5 in Samuel A. Stouffer *et al.*, *Measurement and Prediction*, Vol. 4 in *Studies in Social Psychology in World War II* (Princeton: Princeton University Press, 1950).

Figure 33. *Three Patterns of Scaling Error* [see also p. 126]

Respondent Rank Order	A Random Scale Errors	B Grouped Non-Scale Errors	C Gradient Quasi-Scale Errors
1	X	X	X
2	X	X	X
3	⊗	X	X
4	X	X	X
5	X	X	X
6	X	X	⊗
7	X	X	X
8	⊗	⊗	X
9	X	⊗	⊗
10	X	⊗	⊗
11	X	⊗	X
12	⊗	⊗	X
13	X	X	X
14	X	X	X
15	X	X	⊗
16	X	X	⊗
17	X	X	⊗
18	⊗	X	X
19	X	X	X
20	X	X	X
21	⊗	X	X
22	X	X	X
23	X	X	X
24	X	X	X
25	X	X	X
26	X	X	X
27	X	X	X
28	X	X	X
29	⊗	X	X
30	X	X	X
31	X	X	X
32	X	X	X
33	⊗	X	X
34	X	X	⊗
35	X	X	⊗
36	X	X	⊗
37	X	X	X
38	⊗	X	X
39	X	⊗	X
40	X	⊗	X
41	X	⊗	X
42	X	⊗	X

Figure 33. (*continued*)

Respondent Rank Order	A Random Scale Errors	B Grouped Non-Scale Errors	C Gradient Quasi-Scale Errors
43	⊗	⊗	X
44	X	X	X
45	X	X	X
46	X	X	X
47	X	X	⊗
48	X	X	X
49	X	X	X
50	⊗	X	X

reason, the very randomness of the pattern indicates that rejection of the item will result in a random reordering of the total scores and a consequent random production of new errors.

Item B has a pattern of responses which Suchman calls *grouped non-scale errors*. As in Item A, there are five errors above the cutting point and five errors below the cutting point, but they are grouped rather than being randomly distributed. As Suchman points out:

> The grouping of errors into nonscale types indicates that more than one strong variable (attitude) is present. We cannot find any single rank order of respondents that would successfully represent the attitudes of respondents on both variables.[2]

Item B, therefore, should clearly be rejected. There is no chance that errors with this pattern will disappear as is possible with the random scale errors.

Item C represents the pattern called *gradient quasi-scale errors*. As in Items A and B, there are ten errors in all. The errors are not randomly scattered as in Item A. They are grouped to some extent but in a different manner from Item B. Note that the groups become progressively larger as they move from the top and bottom of the distribution of total scores toward the center. This is related to two important probablistic properties of response patterns. First, as we have already shown in Figure 23, the number of possible nonscale-type response patterns that can result in a particular total score increases for the total scores nearer to the middle of the range of possible scores.[3] Second, in case of a scale using only dichotomous

---

[2] *Ibid.*, p. 160.

[3] The number of non-scale-type response patterns also increases as we increase the total number of items in the scale and the number of response categories, for each item.

items, as in Figure 33, while the number of nonscalable patterns of response for a total score increases toward the middle of the range, the number of *scale-type* response patterns does not increase. Therefore, the *proportion* (of all possible response patterns corresponding to a particular total score) of scale-types decreases as the total scores approach the middle of the range. This also means that the probability of obtaining a scale-type pattern by chance decreases as the total score approaches the middle of the range. Therefore, the gradient quasi-scale error pattern (Column C in Figure 33) is a function of chance rather than the effect of some additional attitude dimension reflected by that item. For this reason the pattern represented in Item C is preferable to that in Item B.

There is an additional pattern of error not represented by any of the three items in Figure 33. This additional pattern might be called the *random non-scale error*. This pattern is illustrated by Item X in Figure 34. Although both items (X and Y) have the same amount of error (6/24 or 25%), Item X should be rejected because the error is randomly distributed around a non-scale pattern, while in Item Y the error is randomly distributed around a scale pattern.[4]

Obviously a pattern resembling that of Item X should be rejected. Under certain conditions it might be advisable to retain Item Y even though it has 25% error, depending upon the application of the second criterion, the item's position on the scale. After we review the four patterns of error, we will turn our attention to this second criterion for the retention or rejection of an item.

In summary, we can rank the four patterns of error in order of desirability (assuming other characteristics of the item are equal) as follows, with number (1) being the best:

(1) Random scale errors
(2) Gradient quasi-scale errors
(3) Grouped non-scale errors
(4) Random non-scale errors

The argument for the superiority of (1) over (2) is not as clear as the argument for the rest of the rankings. Empirically, items having type (1) error patterns usually have fewer errors than those with type (2) patterns.

Unfortunately, in practice errors do not always emerge in a clearly identifiable pattern. They may seem to follow one pattern for part of the range and then switch to another pattern. However, the larger the

---

[4] This comparison in Figure 34 also demonstrates the mathematical fact that the coefficient of reproducibility of an item can never be less than the proportion of responses falling into the most frequently used category of that item regardless of whether or not the item is scalable.

Respondents	X					Y				
	1	2	3	4	5	1	2	3	4	5
1					X					×
2			×							×
3			×						⊗	
4				⊗						×
5			×						×	
6	⊗							⊗		
7			×						×	
8			×						×	
9			×					×		
10			×					×		
11				⊗			⊗			
12			×					×		
13			×				×			
14		⊗					×			
15			×			⊗				
16			×				×			
17			×			×				
18	⊗					×				
19			×				⊗			
20			×			×				
21			×			×				
22					⊗	×				
23			×				⊗			
24			×			×				
Distribution of Error	2	1	0	1	2	1	3	1	1	0
Total Errors	6					6				
Percent error	25%					25%				

Figure 34. *Scalable versus Non-Scalable Error*

number of respondents and the more items in the scale, the more reliably we can identify the different patterns. With only 20 respondents and six items, it is almost impossible to make any reliable distinctions, but if there are 50 respondents and 15 items, there is more chance for the pattern to manifest itself.

Above all, we hope to have demonstrated that there is no necessary simple correspondence between the *amount* of error and the *pattern* of the error and that both should be taken into consideration in deciding which items to reject.

Position of Item on the Scale

If an item producing the largest amount of error happens to be the only item in that position on the scale, it would be undesirable to eliminate it and leave a hole in the range. It is better to tolerate some error and have a complete scale than to eliminate error and have an incomplete scale incapable of validly ranking respondents or of making fine discriminations among respondents. In making this decision one must weigh the effect on the coefficient of reproducibility against the effect on the discrimination power of the scale.

In making this judgment we should keep in mind that there is a tendency for the items that contribute the most error to be in the middle range of the scale. We have already shown this in the explanation of the gradient quasi-scale errors, which tend to increase as we move toward the middle of the range of total scores. Items at the extreme ends of the scale tend to use only two or three of the five response categories. Therefore there is a larger number of responses in each of the categories used than is the case for the items in the middle of the range, which often use all five categories. Since, as I have already pointed out, the coefficient of reproducibility for a single item cannot fall below the maximum percentage of responses falling into any one of the categories, the coefficient of reproducibility tends to be lower in the middle-range items. This is why it would be desirable to retain an item like Y in Figure 34, which uses all five of its response categories, even though the individual item's error of reproducibility is 25%. It would still be possible to keep the total error for all items in the scale below 10%.

If two items occupy the same position on the scale, we can eliminate one without losing power of discrimination and without contributing to a spuriously high coefficient of reproducibility. In this case we decide which of the two to eliminate by applying the first criterion, the pattern of error, and the third criterion, the amount of error. If the items are equal on both criteria, it does not matter which is eliminated. The only benefit in this case is that the questionnaire is shortened and the amount of analysis reduced without any sacrifice of scalability or power of discrimination.

If one of the two items has a smaller amount of error and a good pattern, there is no problem deciding which one to reject. If one has a clearly better pattern but a higher amount of error, it should be retained unless the amount of error exceeds tolerable limits. (Although the "tolerable limit" of error for the whole set of items has been somewhat arbitrarily set at 10%, this is not a guide to the maximum error we should tolerate in a particular item.) The rule limiting the tolerable amount of error in a single item is given later in this chapter.

In the discussion of the item's position on the scale, we did not specify precisely how to determine an item's rank position. This is done by looking at the marginal distributions for each item. In the case of dichotomous item, this is simply the frequency distribution of the numbers of positive and negative answers given to that item by the sample of respondents. To be certain that a set of items covered the full range, we would ideally have to include at least one item which always received a negative response and one item which always received a positive response. Then we would like to have the proportion of positive and negative responses change evenly from one rank order to the next, as in Figure 35.

Since all five items (A, B, C, D, E) are dichotomous, there is only one cutting point in each item. The items are arranged in rank order according to their position on the scale, so the cutting points move

Figure 35. *Response Patterns and Marginal Totals*

	A		B		C		D		E	
	+	−	+	−	+	−	+	−	+	−
			x		x		x		x	
			x		x		x		x	
			x		x		x		x	
			x		x		x		x	
			x		x		x		x	
				x	x		x		x	
				x	x		x		x	
				x	x		x		x	
				x	x		x		x	
				x	x		x		x	
				x		x	x		x	
				x		x	x		x	
				x		x	x		x	
				x		x	x		x	
				x		x	x		x	
				x		x		x	x	
				x		x		x	x	
				x		x		x	x	
				x		x		x	x	
				x		x		x	x	
Number Positive	0		5		10		15		20	
Percent Positive	0		25%		50%		75%		100%	

upward from left to right. Since the items represent equidistant points on the ranked total scores, they progress upward in equal steps; and since each step represents one quartile, or 25%, of the distribution of scores, the cutting points move up in units of five cases (5/20 = 25%).

This conversion of each item's percentage of positive responses into its position on the scale is simple in the case of dichotomous items. With a set of items having five answer categories, we must use some other way of arriving at a single number representing the distribution of responses to each item. This can be done most simply by the method used in scalograms A, B, and C, (Figures 27, 28, and 29). Simply count the frequency of responses (f) in each category; multiply this frequency by the scale value of the corresponding response categories (fx); and add these five products (Σfx) to obtain the scale value for each item. This procedure is shown in rows (a), (b), (c) of scalograms A, B, and C.

If in a particular scalogram there are five answer categories with the assigned scale values of 1, 2, 3, 4, 5 and there are 20 respondents, then we know that the maximum scale value of an item is 100 (5 × 20) and the minimum 20 (1 × 20). If the five answer categories are assigned the values 0, 1, 2, 3, 4, then the maximum scale value of an item is 80 (4 × 20) and the minimum is 0 (0 × 20). Whether the five answer categories are given the values of 1 to 5, 0 to 4, or minus 2 to plus 2 (-2, -1, 0, +1, +2) is immaterial as long as the same system is used for all items.

Using these scale values, then, we can get an idea of how the items are positioned on the scale. Although we can clearly establish their ordinal positions, the interitem distance on that scale is relative only to the rank order of a particular sample of respondents.

In addition to considering the first criterion of the type of error pattern and the second criterion of the scale position of the item, we need to look at the third criterion, the amount of error, which is not necessarily correlated with the first two criteria.

Amount of Error in the Item

If the error pattern and scale position of two items are equal, we simply retain the one with the smaller amount of error. However, there are cases when an item must be rejected despite the fact that it is the only one occupying an important scale position. A general rule of thumb, with theoretical support which we will not present here, is that any item that has more error than non-error (over 50% error) in any category of response should be rejected even though its inclusion might not raise the total error of reproducibility above the 10% mark.

If such an item happens to occupy a needed position on the scale, we may try to salvage it by combining the answer categories in the manner described below, but if this fails to reduce the error below 50% it will have to be rejected.

COMBINING RESPONSE CATEGORIES

Often we can avoid rejecting items by combining answer categories. By inspecting the scalogram we can readily see in which items the error might be reduced by combining categories. When we see the response pattern oscillating between two or more categories rather than forming a solid streak in the column, there is a possibility of improving the scale's coefficient of reproducibility by combining the adjacent categories where the oscillation takes place.

Even if the item is scalable, such an oscillating pattern can occur because of different verbal habits among respondents. For example, on a particular item a certain person might tend to avoid saying "strongly agree" and say simply "agree" because in that context he feels there is no real difference between the two categories, or because he feels for some reason reluctant to take an extreme position.

In other cases this oscillation may take place in the middle categories when the response categories are not of the abstract type (strongly agree to strongly disagree) but are a set of more concrete action alternatives in which the extreme positions are more reliably interpreted and at the inner portion of the range the distinctions are more ambiguous.

In Figure 36 there are response patterns to five items that might benefit from combining answer categories. In item A the oscillation clearly occurs between categories 4 and 5; in item B it is between categories 3 and 4; in item C it is among the inner three categories 2, 3, and 4; in item D there is one oscillation pattern between categories 1 and 2 at the lower end of the range and another between categories 4 and 5 at the upper end of the range; and in item E there is an oscillation between categories 1 and 2 at the lower end of the range and among categories 3, 4, and 5, at the upper end of the range.

These are only examples; other patterns may occur requiring that we combine any number of adjacent categories. Items may have two, three, or four categories remaining after combining.

The question arises in practice as to how much or what pattern of oscillation calls for combining the answer categories for a particular

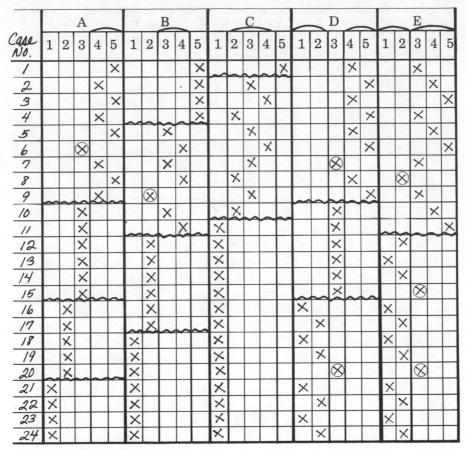

Figure 36. *Combining Response Categories*

item. The answer depends upon the amount of error remaining after we have minimized it in locating the cutting points. *If the amount of error cannot be reduced to less than the amount of non-error by a cutting point, then we should try to combine categories.* The need for combining answer categories is determined for each item independently. Therefore, there may be two to five answer categories for different questions in the scale.

For example, in Item A in Figure 36 the solid streaks in columns 1, 2, and 3 are so clear that there is no problem in placing the cutting point for each. These cutting points result in no errors in columns 1 or 2 and only one error in column 3. However, it is impossible to place the cutting point for columns 4 and 5 in a way that will result in less error than non-error. If the cutting point were drawn between case 1 and case 2, then the responses of cases 3, 5, 6, and 8 become errors. Thus, in column 5 the ratio of errors to non-errors becomes 4:1 when it should be less than 1:1. If we put the cutting point after any case from 2 through 8, we find each time that the amount of error in columns 4 and 5 exceeds the amount of non-error in those two columns.

Similarly, the patterns in items B, C, D, and E in Figure 36 are such that it is impossible to reduce the number of errors below 50% no matter where the cutting points are placed for those columns to be combined.

The rule makes it unnecessary to combine adjacent categories as long as we can establish cutting points which will reduce the error even slightly below the amount of non-error. This may seem at first to be a rather low level of purification of a scale. Why not try to purify by combining those categories where the error is 45%, or 40%, or even 35% instead of only where it exceeds 50%?

First, a certain amount of error will always occur by chance because of the unreliability of responses; therefore, not all the error in a particular item is due to its unscalability. Second, as we will show in the next section, the apparent reduction of error by combining items on the initial scalogram is only tentative; we must test the effects by making up a new scalogram on the basis of new scale values for the combined categories. If the purification of the first scalogram is too drastic, there is a strong probability that no reduction of error will be obtained or even that an increase of error will result in the purified scalogram. This increase might occur not in the purified item but in any or all of the others.

Third, even if there is a gain in the coefficient of reproducibility, there will be some loss in the range of scores and discrimination power of the scale with each loss of an answer category. For these reasons it seems prudent to accept the minimal test of acceptability (less error than non-error) in deciding whether adjacent categories should be combined.

RESCORING THE SCALOGRAM

New errors may appear as a result of an attempt to purify the items because both the rejection of an item and the combination of two or more answer categories always result in new total scores that change the rank order of some of the respondents. Each person's responses must be rescored taking into account both the rejected items and the combined answer categories. Fortunately, this can be done rather quickly from the original scalogram without going back to the individual questionnaires. Once these new totals are obtained, a purified scalogram is made up with the respondents in the new rank order and with the newly assigned scale values recorded for each item. When the new scalogram is completed, the same procedure as was used in the original scalogram is used to calculate the new coefficient of reproducibility.

Rejected Items

Simply cross out the whole item from the first scalogram so that the values of the responses will be omitted in rescoring the response pattern.

Combined Response Categories

Whenever two or more categories have been combined, it is necessary to assign new scale values to some or all of the categories for that particular item. On the original scalogram you should indicate clearly which columns are being combined and what scale value is being assigned to the combination, as shown in Figure 37. On the new scalogram sheet for the purified scores cross out those columns having whichever scale values you no longer need according to your method of rescoring.

New Total Scores

Once the rejected items have been crossed out on the original scalogram and new scale values have been assigned to the combined categories, simply add the new values of the items across in each row to obtain the new score for each respondent. Write this score in the "revised scores" column on the right of the scalogram as shown in Figure 38. When all the respondents have been given their revised scores, inspect the whole column of revised scores to determine their new rank order. Write the new rank order in the final "rank" column at the right. It is crucial that this rank ordering be correct. Note that tie scores are handled by giving the *same* rank number, which is the mean value of rank positions occupied.

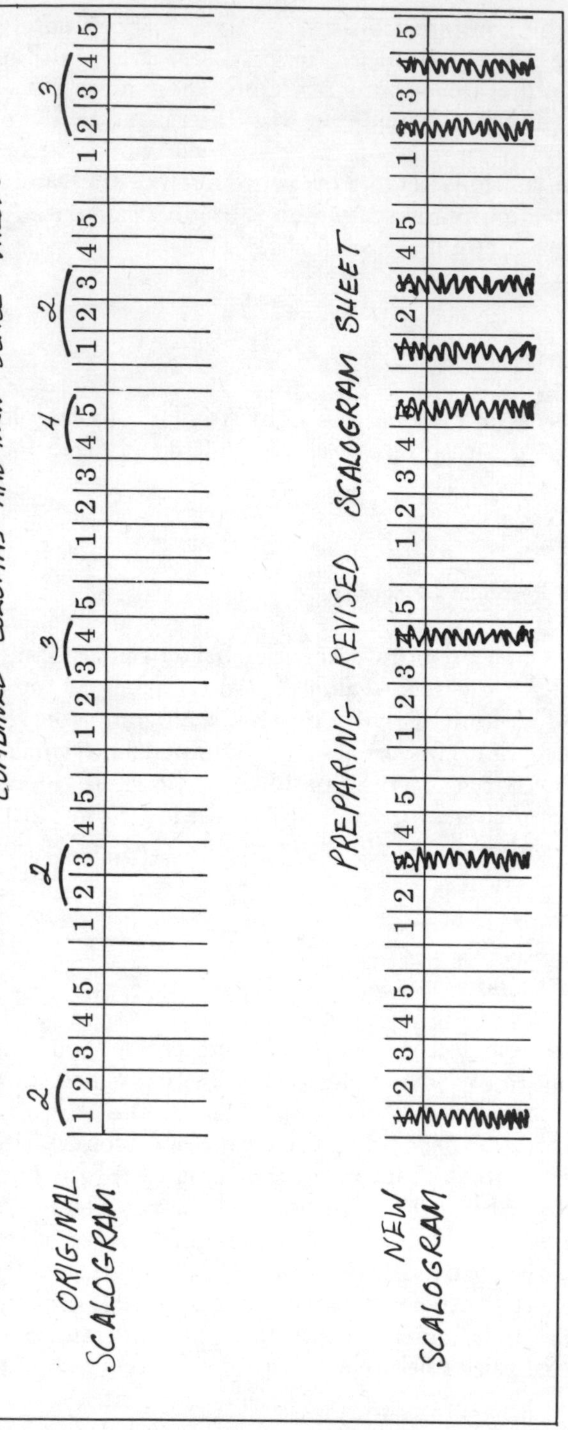

Figure 37. Scoring Combined Categories

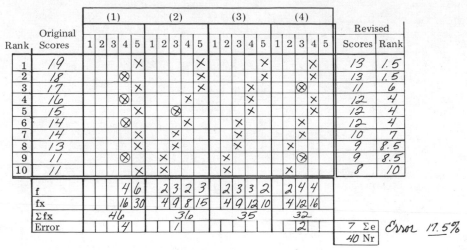

Figure 38. *Rescored Original Scalogram*

Recording Responses of the New Scalogram

After preparing the new scalogram sheet, we can begin recording each respondent's answers as shown in Figure 39. Find the respondent with the highest *revised* score (rank 1) in the original scalogram and write this total score in the top row of the left hand column of the new scalogram.[5] Then record that person's responses in the first row. Continue this process with respondents in the new rank order until all the response patterns have been transferred to the new scalogram. It is advisable after recording each respondent's answers to check the total score by calculating it directly from the X's just entered in the new scalogram to see if it agrees with the new total score.

Recalculating the Coefficient of Reproducibility

Follow the same procedure and principles as in the first scalogram to establish cutting points, counting errors and calculating the coefficient of reproducibility. If you begin with a large enough number of items, it is possible to repeat the purification process, if needed, to reduce the error further. Note that the error of reproducibility was reduced from 17.5% in Figure 38 to only 3.3% in Figure 39.

[5] Within any set of tied ranks it is most convenient to retain the same order as in the original scalogram.

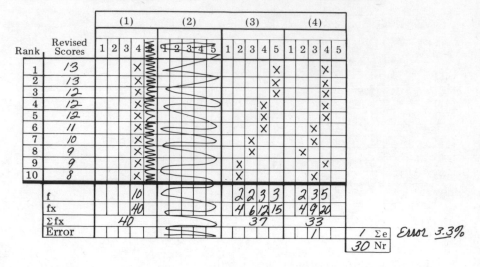

Figure 39. *New Scalogram (Using Revised Total Scores)*

SUMMARY OF STEPS IN SCALOGRAM PROCEDURE

(1) Select the sample of cases to be scaled.
(2) Edit the questionnaires in this sample to eliminate those with missing responses.
(3) Assign scale values to answers on the questionnaire.
(4) Calculate the total score for each case.
(5) Arrange questionnaires in rank order by total scores.
(6) Record the responses on the scalogram sheet.
(7) Calculate the coefficient of reproducibility.
  (a) Choose cutting points.
  (b) Count errors.
  (c) Calculate coefficient of reproducibility.
(8) Purify the scale if needed.
  (a) Reject offending items.
  (b) Combine categories if needed.
(9) Rescore the responses.
  (a) Assign new scale values to combined columns.
  (b) Obtain new total scores.
  (c) Assign new ranks to the total scores.
  (d) Record responses on new scalogram sheet.
(10) Calculate new coefficient of reproducibility.

Laboratory Problem 8 gives you an opportunity to perform steps (8), (9), and (10) without having to repeat any of the previous steps.

This is done by continuing with the data you were analyzing in Laboratory Problem 7.

LABORATORY PROBLEM 8
Purifying the Scale

The error of reproducibility of the unpurified scale in laboratory problem 7 came very close to the acceptable level for a valid unidimensional scale. This would be usable as a quasi-scale without any change, but it is possible to reduce the error of reproducibility either by rejecting some items or by combining certain answer categories in others.

(1) *Rejecting items*: In this scalogram there is *only one* item that clearly should be omitted. Of the three criteria for rejection explained in the text, one (the pattern of error) cannot be applied in this case because the small sample of 30 cases does not allow differences in patterns to emerge clearly.

   Which item should be rejected?

(2) *Combining answer categories*: In this scalogram you should combine categories in *only two* items. In each case two categories should be combined into one. To attempt any more might actually increase the amount of error of reproducibility.

   Which answer categories in which items should be combined? Indicate these combinations on the scalogram sheet and assign new scale values to the combinations.

(3) *Obtain the new total scores and rank orders*: Be careful not to make errors in this rescoring process. The quickest way is to do it slowly and carefully.

   In how many cases did the rank order change as a result of rescoring?

(4) *Transfer the purified data to the new scalogram sheet*: Cross out the items and answer categories not needed on the new scalogram sheet. Transfer the data row by row with the respondents in their new rank order. A blank scalogram sheet can be reproduced from the sample in Appendix A.

   What is the new total number of responses in the scalogram?

(5) *Calculate the new coefficient of reproducibility*: Establish cutting points to minimize errors, count the total number of

errors, divide by the new total number of responses, and multiply by 100 to obtain the percent *error* of reproducibility and subtract from 100% to obtain the new *coefficient* of reproducibility.

What is the new coefficient of reproducibility for the purified scale?

Chapter 6.   Interpreting and Presenting Scales

Interpreting the results of administering attitude scales involves considering nonstatistical criteria of scalability in addition to the co-efficient of reproducibility. Also in some cases additional statistical measures of unidimensionality may be used which are more probaba-listic than the coefficient of reproducibility. Also, in interpreting the results we should have an appreciation of the practical utility of a quasi-scale which does not satisfy the rigorous criterion of 90% re-producibility. Finally, the interpretation of results may in some cases involve a salvage operation, searching for relevance in separate items which have been proved non-scalable as a set.

ADDITIONAL CRITERIA OF SCALABILITY

The entire procedure summarized earlier is a means of arriving at the coefficient of reproducibility. As we explained the procedure, we implied that there were considerations in determining scalability other than simply obtaining the highest possible coefficient of repro-ducibility. Although reproducibility is the most important single criterion, there are at least five others that should be taken into ac-count. These are the range of marginal distributions, the patterns of error, the number of items in the scale, the number of response cate-gories in each item, and the proportion of error to non-error in each item.

Range of Distributions

The position of an item on the scale is indicated by the total value of the response to the item. Thus, for simple dichotomous items rank position on the scale is indicated empirically by the number of positive answers received. In this case the maximum total score is equal to the number of items. In items with three or more answer categories, the value of the group's responses to an item indicates the rank order and something about the scale distance between items.

Although there should be some items at the two extreme ends of the scale, these will have an artificially high reproducibility. The reproducibility of a particular item, as we have noted, can never be less than the percentage of responses falling into a single answer category, regardless of whether or not the set of items constitutes a unidimensional scale, and items at the extremes tend to have a large proportion of responses in a single category. To guard against this spurious reproducibility, we must take care to include items in which the item totals indicate that they fall along the full range, including the middle of the range.

Patterns of Errors

The differences among random scale errors, grouped non-scale errors, and gradient quasi-scale errors have been described and illustrated in Figure 33. We should try to avoid or eliminate the grouped non-scale error patterns and give first preference to the random scale error and second preference to the quasi-scale error. It is often necessary to retain an item with a quasi-scale error pattern if it is needed to fulfill other criteria, such as position on the scale and number of items.

Number of Items

The larger the number of items in a scale, the more significant is a particular coefficient of reproducibility. As the number of items increases, the probability decreases of having a scale-type pattern of response from any individual by chance. It can be demonstrated mathematically that the probability of a spurious scalability drops rapidly with the increase in the number of items.

Another reason for having a larger number of items is that the more items in the scale (assuming the number of responses per item is held constant), the more different total scores can be obtained. This allows us to make finer discriminations and to reduce the number of tie scores. Whether or not fine distinctions are needed depends upon how the total scores are going to be used. If, for example, we need only to place respondents into three ordinal intervals ("high," "medium," and "low"), then the only consideration in determining the number of items would be to represent the full range of the scale and avoid a spuriously high coefficient of reproducibility. On the other hand, if we need to do a Spearman rank correlation between attitudes and some other test score, it would be crucial to make distinctions as fine as possible to avoid having many tied scores. Too many tied scores can make the rank correlation measure inapplicable.

Guttman[1] recommends that 10 or more items should be used to pretest the scalability of the sample of items, but fewer may be used in the larger study provided that the item totals have an appropriate spread and the total scores will make enough distinctions for the purposes at hand.

Number of Response Categories

The same logic that applies to increasing the number of items in the scale also applies to increasing the number of answer categories. Assuming that we hold the number of items constant, any increase in the number of categories increases the number of scale-types, the number of different total scores obtainable, and the power of discrimination of the scale. At the same time it *decreases* the probability of a spuriously high coefficient of correlation.

The number of response categories may range from two to seven depending on the nature of the item and the reliability of the distinctions as shown in the pattern of responses. Even though a questionnaire may have a five-category response to every item, in the scalogram analysis it may be necessary to combine categories so that there is a variation from two to five response categories. This mixture in no way interferes with using the second scalogram to measure the reproducibility.

Proportion of Error to Non-error in Each Item

Even though the coefficient of reproducibility for the whole set of items may be high, it is still necessary to exclude any single item in which the amount of error exceeds the amount of non-error.

[1] Samuel A. Stouffer *et al.*, *Measurement and Prediction*, Vol. 4 in *Studies in Social Psychology in World War II* (Princeton: Princeton University Press, 1950), p. 79.

OTHER STATISTICAL MEASURES
OF REPRODUCIBILITY

In view of the relevance of these additional factors to the real scalability of a set of items, there have been several attempts to develop a new mathematical measure of reproducibility that, unlike the Guttman coefficient of reproducibility, would simultaneously take into account the marginal distribution, the number of items, the number of response categories, and the differences in patterns of errors.

Thus far we have found none of these measures flexible enough to apply to items with more than dichotomous answer categories. An excellent summary of a variety of measures applicable to dichotomous items is given by White and Saltz.[2]

VALUES OF QUASI-SCALES

Although it has become traditional to say that a set of items must have a Guttman coefficient of reproducibility of 90% and must fulfill the four additional criteria of scalability in order to be a true unidimensional scale, in practice it is often very difficult and costly to achieve all of these requirements simultaneously.

It is not necessary to reject a set of scale items as useless simply because they do not achieve the 90% level of reproducibility. If the other criteria are met, and particularly if the errors are either of the random scale pattern or the gradient quasi-scale pattern, the coefficient of reproducibility may be as low as 60%. Still, the total scores would rank the respondents in almost the same rank order; therefore the correlation of the total scores with outside variables will be high. As Suchman explains the quasi scale is very useful:

> The importance of a quasi-scale lies in how it is used for external prediction problems. While we cannot derive a person's responses from his quasi-scale score, the score does yield a zero-order correlation with any outside variable which is equivalent to the multiple correlation on all the items in the quasi-scale. The prediction of the external variable rests essentially on the dominant factor that is being measured by the quasi-scale scores. Thus a quasi scale has the full mathematical advantage of a scalable area.[3]

[2] Benjamin W. White and Eli Saltz, "Measurement of Reproducibility," in Gary M. Maranell (ed.), *Scaling: A Sourcebook for Behavioral Scientists* (Chicago: Aldine Publishing Co., 1974), pp. 172–96.

[3] Edward A. Suchman, "The Utility of Scalogram Analysis," Chapter 5, p. 162, in Samuel A. Stouffer *et al.*, *Measurement and Prediction*, Vol. 4 in *Studies in Social Psychology in World War II* (Princeton: Princeton University Press, 1950).

He points out, further, that reliably ranking respondents in a stable order according to their total scores requires a larger number of quasi-scale items than of true-scale items in which the errors are random and usually in actual practice turn out to be fewer than in the quasi-scale items:

> While the single dominant variable of a quasi-scale cannot be represented by means of a small number of items due to the amount of error involved, increasing the number of items which contain this dominant variable makes this error assume a gradient pattern, and permits an invariant rank order.[4]

Thus, it is defensible to use a set of items fulfilling the criteria of a quasi-scale as a reliable index to an attitude even though the coefficient of reproducibility is very low.

REASONS FOR NON-SCALABILITY

In any attempt to build a Guttman scale there is a possibility that the set of items used will not constitute either a scale or a quasi-scale. First, we will examine some of the reasons why this might be the case; then we will make some suggestions for salvaging information from individual items even though they have clearly been proved to be non-scalable.

No Such Attitude in the Population

It is possible to try to measure an attitude which does not exist in reality. Theoretically human beings at some time or place could have an attitude toward valve cores, horseshoe nails, starfish, stairstep pyramids, the word "the," or any other thing or idea we can name or define. However, whether or not such an attitude exists in a certain population at a given moment is a question to be determined empirically.

Even the fact that a certain set of items comprised a unidimensional scale for a particular population on a particular day does not guarantee that the same items will be scalable a month later. Attitudes in a population are like the images on the lumia screen. They form, change shape, sharpen their definition, shrink, expand, dissolve, and disappear. Some attitudes form and dissolve quickly while others linger for decades or centuries. For example, the Bogardus Social Distance Scale, which is essentially a measure of attitudes toward

[4] *Ibid.*, p. 163.

racial, religious, and national minorities, has shown that the U.S. population in general has changed very little between 1924 and 1974 in these respects. At the other extreme, a teenager's attitude toward a rock singer may form and dissolve in a matter of weeks.

It is important to distinguish between changes in people's position on an attitude scale and historic shifts in the objects of attitude. In the first case the repeated use of a Guttman scale would continue to demonstrate unidimensionality while the mean score of a sample of the population would shift. In the second case the set of items would become non-scalable.

Something which is an object of attitude in the minds of the researchers may not be an object of attitude in the population to be sampled. This is the basic reason for the invention of Guttman scaling. It does not assume that anything the researcher believes to be an object of social attitudes is in fact so. Instead, it allows us to test whether such an attitude exists at this time in the population sampled.

Items Do Not Sample Attitude Content

In the beginning of this book, we stressed the problems of discovering, constructing, and selecting items relevant to a particular attitude. Not only must there in fact be an attitude toward a given social object, but also the specific items must be associated with the feeling toward that object.

With change in time, the same items may change their meaning because of a shift in the general socio-cultural context in which the testing is taking place. The specific ways in which an attitude may be expressed toward an object may change over time, but the essential feeling dimension may remain. For example, a negative attitude toward war may be expressed in different rhetoric, vocabulary, and style by different age groups at a given time or by the same group at different times.

A set of items may contain several items related to the content area of a given attitude and may still prove to be unscalable. The content of some of the items could be related to a different attitude, or an item could be "double-barreled," containing stimuli for two different attitudes, or capable of a dual interpretation, stimulating different attitudes.

So, even though an attitude exists in the population in question, we must find the proper verbal content to spark a feeling response related to only one attitudinal dimension.

Items Have No Proper Calibration

Even though the qualitative content of all items in the set may be relevant, they may fail to scale because the calibration is not correct. For example, if all the items occupy the same position on the scale, there is little chance of demonstrating unidimensionality. Also, if the answer categories are such that the relative ordinal value of the categories in ambiguous and unreliable, there will be an undue amount of error of reproducibility.

All three conditions (existence of an attitude, proper unidimensional content in the items, and proper metric considerations) must be fulfilled by a set of items if they are to show scalability. Even if a set proves to be non-scalable, this may not mean that all is lost since much information can be salvaged from responses to the individual questions.

PRESENTING THE RESULTS OF AN ATTITUDE SCALE

After you have developed the scale, obtained the responses of a sample of the target population, measured the reproducibility, and purified the items to improve the reproducibility, you are ready to present your findings to the interested audience. The suggestions offered here assume that you are making the simplest type of report, in which you present the responses of the sample to only one attitude scale, without relating these attitudes to other variables. Not all the suggestions given below apply to every report of results; their applicability depends upon whether the items are proved to be scalable and how the results are to be used.

Methodology

To make the findings clear to the reader of the report, certain points on the methodology should be included. Whether they should be a central feature in the text or relegated to footnotes or an appendix depends upon the audience and purpose of the report.

Name and Define the Attitude. It helps the reader to have a clear picture at the outset of the attitude you are attempting to measure. This can be done by first giving the attitude an appropriate descriptive label, then describing the object of the attitude and the nature of the relationship between the respondent and the object that you intend to measure. For example:

Label: "Legitimacy of Political Violence on Campus"

Definition: Here violence is construed to include covert threats as well as overt acts of violence. It includes only those forms of violence used to settle disputes between administrators, faculty, other employees, and students, and which take place on the college campus or other property belonging to the college. We are interested in measuring the extent to which students feel that this "political violence" is a *legitimate means* for settling these disputes.

By considering both the *object* of the attitude and the particular dimension of the respondent's *relationship* to that object, we can consciously rule out other possible subject-object relationships. For example, the definition above rules out several other possible relationships between the students and violence, such as the extent to which the student is frightened by violence on the campus, the extent to which the student himself would be willing to use violence, or the extent to which the student feels that particular instances of violence have been effective. Of course, all these different dimensions might have some functional relationship to the dimension we are trying to measure, but that relationship is another problem.

By clearly delineating the object (violence) and putting it into a specific situational context, we rule out many other objects which could have fallen into the category designated by the label "Violence on the Campus" such as rapes, muggings, fistfights over personal matters, suicides, etc.

It is not always possible to clearly separate the object from the relevant dimension of the respondents' relationship to the object, but a serious attempt to do it *before* selecting and constructing items for the scale will increase the probability of obtaining a set of scalable items. In presenting the results of the study the same conceptual separation helps the reader to understand more clearly the dimension measured by the set of items presented.

Describe Respondents.   You should show, if it is not completely obvious, the relationship between the object of attitude and the respondent. If certain *characteristics* of the respondents, such as role, age, sex, ethnicity, social class, educational level, or religion, are relevant to the type of population from which the respondents were sampled, this should be specified. The particular slant and wording of the attitude items make more sense to the reader when he knows the sample for whom the items were designed.

If the *time* and *place* at which this population was sampled is relevant to the problem, this should also be made clear.

The extent to which the respondents constituted a *representative sample* of some population should also be specified, including the sampling method used, the original size of the sample, and the proportion of the sample who actually responded.

Adequacy of the Scale.   In discussing the adequacy of the scale, you should give the *error of reproducibility*, the number of items on the original scale that had to be *eliminated* as irrelevant to the dimension, the amount of *collapsing* of answer categories you did, and whether the amount of *error between cutting points* in the Guttman analysis was always less than the amount of non-error.

Also, if there is evidence that the scale was too short on either the positive or the negative end this should be mentioned. Ideally, there should be one item at the upper end of the scale for which every respondent checked the answer having the lowest scale value and one item at the lower end of the scale for which every respondent checked the answer having the highest scale value. If you have any strong reason to suspect that this set of items, even though scalable for this sample of respondents, might not be scalable with respondents at another time or place, this should be discussed.

Presenting the Findings

If There Is No Scale.   If the Guttman analysis shows that your dreams of a unidimensional scale have been shattered, do not despair. Remember that each question standing alone still yields information about the respondents' relationship to the social object in question. Also, in some cases the responses to a single question constitute a crude but helpful mini-scale and can be used in some measures of association with other variables.

If There Is a Scale.   If there is a scalable set of items, you should show not only how the total scores on the scale relate to other relevant variables involved in the particular study but also how the total scores for your sample of respondents are distributed along the possible range of total scores. It is also helpful, regardless of whether the items are scalable, to show how the respondents are distributed among the answer choices to *each item* separately.

Distribution of Total Scores

If the sample is very small (under 30), the distribution of scores can be shown. Simply list them in rank order just as they were in the final revision of the scalogram. The total possible range of the scale should be given. The same data could be presented in a frequency table or bar graph, which presents the scores in groups. Figure 40 shows three ways of presenting the distribution of the same total scores: an array, a frequency table, and a bar graph.

When the sample is small, either the array or the frequency table can be used effectively. Grouping has an advantage in that, even with a very small sample, it gives a more graphic picture of the distribution of total scores in relationship to the maximum possible range permitted by the scale. For example, the graph immediately demonstrates that none of the respondents in the sample fell into the lowest quarter of the range and that the modal response was in the next to the top quarter of the range. The array has some advantages. It gives the additional information that no one in the sample had the maximum score of 40 and no one had a score below 24. However, arrays lose their value as the number in the sample becomes large.

Distributions on Individual Items

If the items comprize a scalable set, it is helpful to the reader if the items are arranged in *rank order* from the most anti to the most pro statements even though they may have been in a scrambled order in the questionnaire. In this way the reader can get a feel of the rationale behind the unidimensionality. You should *omit the non-scalable items* from this list and also *combine the answer categories* as you did to obtain the coefficient of reproducibility reported. Even though the original attitude questionnaire may have provided five response categories, some items may have had their answers collapsed into four, three, or even two categories, as shown below:

Original Questionnaire	Collapsed to Four
1–Strongly agree	1–Agree
2–Agree	2–Undecided
3–Undecided	3–Disagree
4–Disagree	4–Strongly disagree
5–Strongly disagree	

Collapsed to Three	Collapsed to Two
1–Agree	1–Agree or undecided
2–Undecided	2–Disagree
3–Disagree	

Figure 40. *Three Ways of Presenting the Distribution of the Same Total Scores on Political-Violence Attitude Scale*

ARRAY

Range: 12 (*anti*)
through 40 (*pro*)

38	28
37	27
36	27
36	27
34	26
33	26
32	26
32	25
31	25
30	24

FREQUENCY TABLE

Range: 12 (*anti*) through 40 (*pro*)

Total score	f	%
12–18	0	15
19–25	3	15
26–32	11	55
33–40	6	30
Total	20	100

BAR GRAPH

Range: 12 (*anti*) through 40 (*pro*)

Total Score

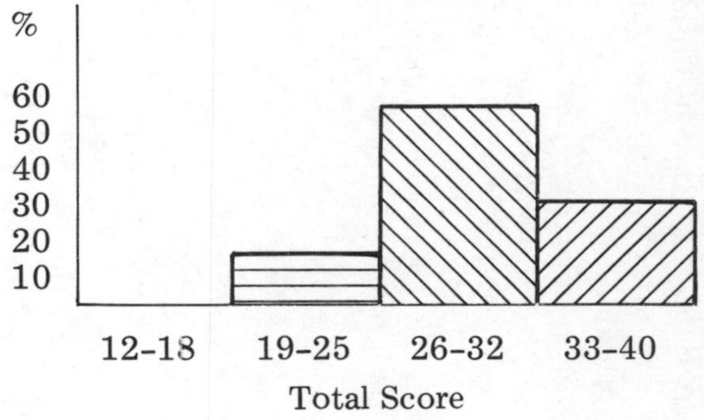

If the set of items proves to be unscalable, there is no need to collapse answer categories when presenting the distribution of responses to the separate items. Also, there is no particular rank order for presenting the set of non-scalable items.

The clearest presentation of the distribution of responses to the separate items can be made by putting the statement in quotes with the distribution immediately under it. The distribution may be shown either as raw frequencies as a percentage distribution, or both. In any case the *totals* should be given at the bottom, as shown in Figure 41.

Interpreting the Meaning of the Results

Although it is important to present the methodology and the findings honestly, completely, and accurately, it is equally important for the person who did the study to interpret the meaning of the data in relationship to the original purpose of the study. The complexity of the interpretation will depend upon whether the purpose was simply to describe the amount of a certain attitude in a given population, to

Figure 41. *Reporting Distribution of Responses to a Single Item*

(1) "I think that all atheists ought to be put in jail."

	f	%
Agree	12	25
Undecided	12	25
Disagree	24	50
Total	48	100%

(2) "Atheists should not be allowed to teach in schools or universities."

	f	%
Strongly agree	8	16.7
Agree	12	25.0
Undecided	12	25.0
Disagree	16	33.3
Strongly disagree	0	0.0
Total	48	100.0%

compare one population with another, or to study the relationships between attitude and some other variables in one or more populations.

If measures of central tendency of the distribution of attitude scores are needed, use those appropriate to ordinal data, such as the median (rather than the mean), quartiles, deciles, or percentiles. If it is appropriate to measure the amount of association between the attitude and any other variable, it is necessary to use statistical techniques appropriate to either nominal or ordinal data (Chi square, Rho, Tschuprow's T^2, Yule's Q, etc.) rather than those appropriate only to interval scale data. This would be the case even if the second variable we want to associate with attitude is an interval scale variable. As long as one of the two variables is ordinal, we must use ordinal measures by converting both variables to ranks.

In addition to using appropriate statistical models for searching for meaningful relationships, the researcher should not shy away from contributing more impressionistic or unsystematic observations which might throw light upon the meaning of the relationships that are demonstrated statistically. Of course we must refrain from confusing flights of fancy with educated guesses and insightful observations.

Epilogue

We began with an attempt to convince the reader that quantification of social and psychological phenomena is a common-sense tendency demonstrated by the most casual observation of daily conversations, which abound in quantitative words and phrases—better or worse, happier, smarter, more democratic, more centralized, less efficient.

However, if we want to translate these commonsense expressions into reliable, valid, and accurate scientific procedures and results, we must grasp the basic concepts of quantification to distinguish between the process of enumerating objects or events and measuring some property of objects or events. If we are not counting but measuring, we must plunge into scaling theory. Once we understand whether we are dealing with a nominal, ordinal, interval, or ratio scale, we can more fully understand the operational manifestations of unidimensionality and the procedures for calibrating the scale.

Assuming that you have been able to follow the detailed procedures, that you have completed the laboratory problems as you went along, and that you will review the theoretical concepts, you should have a firm enough grasp of the essentials to apply them to problems you choose for the measurement of a social-psychological force such as attitude or for the establishment of hierarchical structures or chronological processes.

If you need inspiration and encouragement at some time, it might be helpful to examine some of the scales reported in other studies or in collections of scales like Bonjean's and Miller's, cited in the bibliography.

Don't be disheartened if your first attempt to build a scale does not pass the rigorous Guttman test of unidimensionality. Remember that whatever attitude, hierarchical arrangement, or process you may conjure up in your imagination does not necessarily exist. Nor should you become prematurely confident if your first attempt is an unqualified success since there is always an element of luck involved.

In any case, you will find that having a clear understanding of the concepts, procedures, and values of scaling will open up many opportunities to do more valid, reliable, and accurate measurements of social and psychological properties previously regarded as intangible, imponderable, or unfathomable if not completely inscrutable.

Appendix A. Blank Forms and Data

Figure A-1. *Answer Sheet for All Laboratory Problems*

Name _____

Problem 1

__ (1) __ (2) __ (3) __ (4) __ (5) __ (6) __ (7) __ (8) __ (9) __(10)
__(11) __(12) __(13) __(14) __(15) __(16) __(17) __(18) __(19) __(20)

Problem 2

__ (1) __ (2) __ (3) __ (4) __ (5) __ (6) __ (7) __ (8) __ (9) __(10)
__(11) __(12) __(13) __(14) __(15) __(16) __(17) __(18) __(19) __(20)

Problem 3 Hand in one example of each of the five facet types.

__ (1) __ (2) __ (3) __ (4) __ (5) __ (6) __ (7) __ (8) __ (9) __(10)
__(11) __(12) __(13) __(14) __(15) __(16) __(17) __(18) __(19) __(20)

Problem 4

__ (1) __ (2) __ (3) __ (4) __ (5) __ (6) __ (7) __ (8) __ (9) __(10)

Problem 5

　　Hand in carbon copy of a report containing (1) your definition of the attitude, (2) definition of the relevant population, (3) your 10 constructed items arranged in scale order from the most pro to the most anti.

Problem 6

　　(1) Numbers of the items needing reversal of response codes_____
　　(2) Record your predicted scaleorder here.

Questionnaire item	1	2	3	4	5	6	7	8	9	10
Predicted order										

　　(3) Hand in the completed DATA SUMMARY SHEET.
　　(4) Hand in the completed SCALOGRAM SHEET.

Problem 7

　　(1) Error of reproducibility. Estimated _____ Actual _____
　　(2) Record the actual scale order here.

Questionnaire item	1	2	3	4	5	6	7	8	9	10
Actual order										

　　(3) Hand in SCALOGRAM SHEET? (If the instructor wants to see your scalogram analysis sheet, it must be returned to you before you can do Problem 8 unless you submit a xerox copy.)

Problem 8

　　(1) Number of the rejected item. _____
　　(2) Categories to be combined: Item _____, categories _____; Item _____, cat. _____
　　(3) Number of pairs of cases with rank order reversed. _____
　　(4) New total number of response in scalogram. _____
　　(5) New coefficient of reproducibility. _____
　　(6) Hand in your SCALOGRAM SHEET.

156

Figure A-2. *Summary Answer Sheet*

Laboratory Problem _____   Date _____

Student	Items in Laboratory Problem																				Number Right
	1	2	3	4	5	6	7	8	9	10	11	12	13	14	15	16	17	18	19	20	
1																					
2																					
3																					
4																					
5																					
6																					
7																					
8																					
9																					
10																					
11																					
12																					
13																					
14																					
15																					
16																					
17																					
18																					
19																					
20																					
21																					
22																					
23																					
24																					
25																					
26																					
27																					
28																					
29																					
30																					
Number Wrong																					

Figure A-3. *Data Sheet for Laboratory Problem 6*

Respondents (N = 20)	Items in Questionnaire Order										Total Score	Rank
	1	2	3	4	5	6	7	8	9	10		
Anne	4	5	2	5	2	1	1	1	1	1		
Betty	5	5	5	5	5	3	5	2	4	3		
Charlotte	5	5	5	5	4	1	3	1	3	1		
Donald	4	5	3	5	3	1	2	1	1	1		
Elwood	5	5	4	5	4	1	3	1	2	1		
Frieda	4	5	2	5	1	1	1	1	1	1		
Greg	5	5	3	5	4	1	2	1	1	1		
Harry	5	5	5	5	5	3	5	2	5	3		
Irene	5	5	5	4	5	4	5	3	5	5		
James	4	5	3	5	2	1	1	1	1	1		
Karen	5	5	5	5	4	1	3	1	2	1		
Lorraine	5	5	5	5	5	2	5	1	4	2		
Marty	5	4	5	3	5	4	5	4	5	5		
Nancy	5	5	4	5	4	1	2	1	1	1		
Oliver	5	5	5	5	5	1	4	1	4	1		
Peter	5	5	3	5	3	1	2	1	1	1		
Quincy	4	5	3	5	3	1	1	1	1	1		
Ray	5	5	4	5	4	1	2	1	2	1		
Steve	5	3	5	3	5	5	5	4	5	5		
Tom	5	5	5	4	5	3	5	3	5	4		
Total Value											528	
Rank												

Figure A-4. *Short Scalogram Form for Laboratory Problem 6*

Name ____________________

QUESTIONNAIRE ITEMS

RANK	CASE	Item	1					3					5					7					9					10					6					8					4					2				
		Order	(1)					(2)					(3)					(4)					(5)					(6)					(7)					(8)					(9)					(10)				
		Score	1	2	3	4	5	1	2	3	4	5	1	2	3	4	5	1	2	3	4	5	1	2	3	4	5	1	2	3	4	5	1	2	3	4	5	1	2	3	4	5	1	2	3	4	5	1	2	3	4	5
1	S	45					X					X					X					X					X					X					X				X				X					X		
2																																																					
3																																																					
4																																																					
5																																																					
6																																																					
7																																																					
8																																																					
9																																																					
10																																																					
11																																																					
12																																																					
13																																																					
14																																																					
15																																																					
16																																																					
17																																																					
18																																																					
19																																																					
20	F	14				X			X				X					X					X					X					X					X					X					X				

Figure A-5. *Scalogram Data for Laboratory Problem 7*

Attitude ______ Researchers ______

✓ Original   Error of reproducibility ____%

____ Purified

QUESTIONNAIRE ITEMS

RANK	CASE	SCORE	(1) 1	2	3	4	5	(2) 1	2	3	4	5	(3) 1	2	3	4	5	(4) 1	2	3	4	5	(5) 1	2	3	4	5	(6) 1	2	3	4	5	(7) 1	2	3	4	5	(8) 1	2	3	4	5	(9) 1	2	3	4	5	(10) 1	2	3	4	5	Revised Scores	Revised Rank
1		47					X					X					X					X					X					X					X					X				X				X				
2		46					X					X					X					X					X					X				X						X				X				X				
3		46					X					X					X					X					X				X						X					X					X		X					
4		44					X					X					X					X					X				X						X				X					X			X					
5		43					X					X					X					X				X					X						X					X				X		X						
6		40					X					X					X					X				X				X						X					X				X				X					
7		39					X					X					X				X			X							X					X						X			X				X					
8		38					X					X					X					X		X						X					X							X			X				X					
9		38				X						X				X						X				X				X					X							X			X				X					
10		37					X					X					X				X				X						X				X						X				X			X						
11		36				X					X						X					X		X							X					X					X				X			X						
12		35					X				X						X					X		X							X				X						X			X				X						
13		34					X				X					X						X				X				X				X							X			X				X						
14		33					X				X						X				X				X					X				X							X			X				X						
15		32					X				X						X				X				X					X			X								X			X				X						
16		32					X				X						X				X					X				X			X						X					X				X						
17		31				X					X						X			X					X						X		X							X				X				X						
18		30					X				X					X				X						X				X			X							X			X					X						
19		30					X				X				X						X					X					X		X						X				X					X						
20		29				X					X					X				X					X					X			X							X			X						X					
21		29					X			X						X					X				X						X		X						X				X					X						
22		28					X				X						X			X				X						X			X						X				X					X						
23		27					X				X					X				X					X				X				X						X				X					X						
24		26					X				X					X				X					X				X				X						X				X					X						
25		25					X				X					X				X				X					X				X					X					X						X					
26		24					X			X					X					X				X						X			X						X				X					X						
27		23					X				X				X				X						X				X				X					X					X					X						
28		22					X				X				X					X			X						X				X					X					X					X						
29		22					X			X					X					X				X					X				X					X					X					X						
30		20				X				X					X				X					X					X				X					X					X					X						
		f				5	25																																																
		fx				20	125																																																
		Σfx	145																																																				
		Error																																																				Σe	
																																																					Nr	

Figure A-6. *Scalogram Form for Laboratory Problem 8.*

Attitude ______________________ Researchers ______________

____

____

____ Original

Error of reproducibility _____%

✓ Purified

QUESTIONNAIRE ITEMS

RANK	CASE	SCORE	(1)					(2)					(3)					(4)					(5)					(6)					(7)					(8)					(9)					(10)					Revised	
			1	2	3	4	5	1	2	3	4	5	1	2	3	4	5	1	2	3	4	5	1	2	3	4	5	1	2	3	4	5	1	2	3	4	5	1	2	3	4	5	1	2	3	4	5	1	2	3	4	5	Scores	Rank
1																																																					
2																																																					
3																																																					
4																																																					
5																																																					
6																																																					
7																																																					
8																																																					
9																																																					
10																																																					
11																																																					
12																																																					
13																																																					
14																																																					
15																																																					
16																																																					
17																																																					
18																																																					
19																																																					
20																																																					
21																																																					
22																																																					
23																																																					
24																																																					
25																																																					
26																																																					
27																																																					
28																																																					
29																																																					
30																																																					
		f																																																				
		fx																																																				
		Σfx																																																				
		Error																																																			Σe	
																																																				Nr	

Figure A–7. Scalogram Form for Own Scale.

Appendix B. Solutions to Laboratory Problems

Figure B-1. *Completed Answer Sheet for All Laboratory Problems*

Problem 1

$\underline{}$ (1) $\underline{4}$ (2) $\underline{}$ (3) $\underline{5}$ (4) $\underline{}$ (5) $\underline{}$ (6) $\underline{1}$ (7) $\underline{}$ (8) $\underline{}$ (9) $\underline{}$ (10)
$\underline{1}$ (11) $\underline{2}$ (12) $\underline{}$ (13) $\underline{}$ (14) $\underline{}$ (15) $\underline{3}$ (16) $\underline{}$ (17) $\underline{2}$ (18) $\underline{}$ (19) $\underline{}$ (20)

Problem 2

$\underline{5}$ (1) $\underline{4}$ (2) $\underline{3}$ (3) $\underline{6}$ (4) $\underline{1}$ (5) $\underline{1}$ (6) $\underline{3}$ (7) $\underline{2}$ (8) $\underline{4}$ (9) $\underline{5}$ (10)
$\underline{1}$ (11) $\underline{3}$ (12) $\underline{2}$ (13) $\underline{3}$ (14) $\underline{1}$ (15) $\underline{5}$ (16) $\underline{4}$ (17) $\underline{3}$ (18) $\underline{2}$ (19) $\underline{2}$ (20)

Problem 3 Hand in one example of each of the five face types.

$\underline{5}$ (1) $\underline{4}$ (2) $\underline{3}$ (3) $\underline{2}$ (4) $\underline{1}$ (5) $\underline{1}$ (6) $\underline{5}$ (7) $\underline{2}$ (8) $\underline{4}$ (9) $\underline{3}$ (10)
$\underline{1}$ (11) $\underline{2}$ (12) $\underline{3}$ (13) $\underline{4}$ (14) $\underline{5}$ (15) $\underline{5}$ (16) $\underline{1}$ (17) $\underline{4}$ (18) $\underline{2}$ (19) $\underline{3}$ (20)

Problem 4

$\underline{1}$ (1) $\underline{2}$ (2) $\underline{4}$ (3) $\underline{6}$ (4) $\underline{8}$ (5) $\underline{10}$ (6) $\underline{3}$ (7) $\underline{5}$ (8) $\underline{7}$ (9) $\underline{9}$ (10)

Problem 5

Hand in carbon copy of a report containing (1) your definition of the attitude, (2) definition of the relevant population, (3) your 10 constructed items arranged in scale order from the most pro to the most anti.

Problem 6

(1) Questionnaire items needing reversal of response codes __2 and 4__
(2) Record your predicted scaleorder here.

Questionnaire item	1	2	3	4	5	6	7	8	9	10
Predicted order	1	10	2	9	3	7	4	8	5	6

This is the actual order with which to compare students' predictions

(3) Hand in the completed DATA SUMMARY SHEET.
(4) Hand in the completed SCALOGRAM SHEET.

Problem 7

(1) Error of reproducibility. Estimated _____ · Actual __15%__
(2) Record the actual scale order here.

Questionnaire item	1	2	3	4	5	6	7	8	9	10
Actual order	1	3	2	4	7	5	8	6	9	10

(3) Hand in SCALOGRAM SHEET? (If the instructor wants to see your scalogram analysis sheet, it must be returned to you before you can do Problem 8 unless you submit a xerox copy.

Problem 8

(1) Number of the one rejected item. __5__
(2) Categories to be combined: Item __1__, categories __4&5__ ; Item __6__, cat. __3&4__
(3) Number of new total scores out of rank order. __4__
(4) New total number of response in scalogram. __270__
(5) New coefficient of reproducibility. __90.75% (9.25% error)__
(6) Hand in your SCALOGRAM SHEET.

SOLUTION

Figure B-2. *Completed Data Sheet for Laboratory Problem 6*

Respondents (N = 20)	Items in Questionnaire Order										Total Score	Rank
	1	2	3	4	5	6	7	8	9	10		
Anne	4 /5	2	/5	2	1	1	1	1	1		15	19
Betty	5 /5	5	/5	5	3	5	2	4	3		34	6
Charlotte	5 /5	5	/5	4	1	3	1	3	1		25	9
Donald	4 /5	3	/5	3	1	2	1	1	1		18	16
Elwood	5 /5	4	/5	4	1	3	1	2	1		23	11
Frieda	4 /5	2	/5	1	1	1	1	1	1		14	20
Greg	5 /5	3	/5	4	1	2	1	1	1		20	14
Harry	5 /5	5	/5	5	3	5	2	5	3		35	5
Irene	5 /5	5	24	5	4	5	3	5	5		40	3
James	4 /5	3	/5	2	1	1	1	1	1		16	18
Karen	5 /5	5	/5	4	1	3	1	2	1		24	10
Lorraine	5 /5	5	/5	5	2	5	1	4	2		31	7
Marty	5 24	5	3	5	4	5	4	5	5		43	2
Nancy	5 /5	4	/5	4	1	2	1	1	1		21	13
Oliver	5 /5	5	/5	5	1	4	1	4	1		28	8
Peter	5 /5	3	/5	3	1	2	1	1	1		19	15
Quincy	4 /5	3	/5	3	1	1	1	1	1		17	17
Ray	5 /5	4	/5	4	1	2	1	2	1		22	12
Steve	5	3	5	3	5	5	5	4	5	5	45	1
Tom	5 /5	5	24	5	3	5	3	5	4		38	4
Total Value	95	23	81	26	78	37	62	32	54	40	528	
Rank	1	10	2	9	3	7	4	8	5	6		

Figure B-3. Completed Scalogram for Laboratory Problem 6

SOLUTION

QUESTIONNAIRE ITEMS

Item-number header (with item rank in parentheses) and response sub-columns 1–5:

Item	1 (1)	3 (2)	5 (3)	7 (4)	9 (5)	10 (6)	6 (7)	8 (8)	4 (9)	2 (10)
Rank	—	—	—	—	—	—	—	—	—	—

Left-hand identification columns (RANK / CASE / Score) and the response (1–5) marked with an X for each questionnaire item:

Rank	Case	Score	1 (1)	3 (2)	5 (3)	7 (4)	9 (5)	10 (6)	6 (7)	8 (8)	4 (9)	2 (10)
1	S	45	5	5	5	5	5	5	5	5	4	3
2	M	43	5	5	5	5	5	5	5	5	4	3
3	I	40	5	5	5	5	5	5	5	4	4	1
4	T	38	5	5	5	5	5	5	4	4	3	
5	H	35	5	5	5	5	5	4	4	3	3	
6	B	34	5	5	5	5	4	4	4	3	2	
7	L	31	5	5	5	5	4	4	3	2	1	
8	O	28	5	5	5	4	3	3	2	1	1	
9	C	25	5	5	4	3	3	2	1	1	1	
10	K	24	5	5	4	3	2	2	1	1	1	
11	E	23	5	4	4	3	2	1	1	1	1	
12	R	22	4	4	3	3	2	1	1	1	1	
13	N	21	5	4	3	2	1	1	1	1	1	
14	G	20	5	3	3	2	1	1	1	1	1	
15	P	19	5	3	2	1	1	1	1	1	1	
16	D	18	4	3	2	1	1	1	1	1	1	
17	Q	17	4	2	2	1	1	1	1	1	1	
18	J	16	4	2	1	1	1	1	1	1	1	
19	A	15	4	1	1	1	1	1	1	1	1	
20	F	14	4	1	1	1	1	1	1	1	1	

Figure B-4. Scalogram Analysis for Laboratory Problem 7

Figure B-5. *Scalogram Analysis for Laboratory Problem 8.*

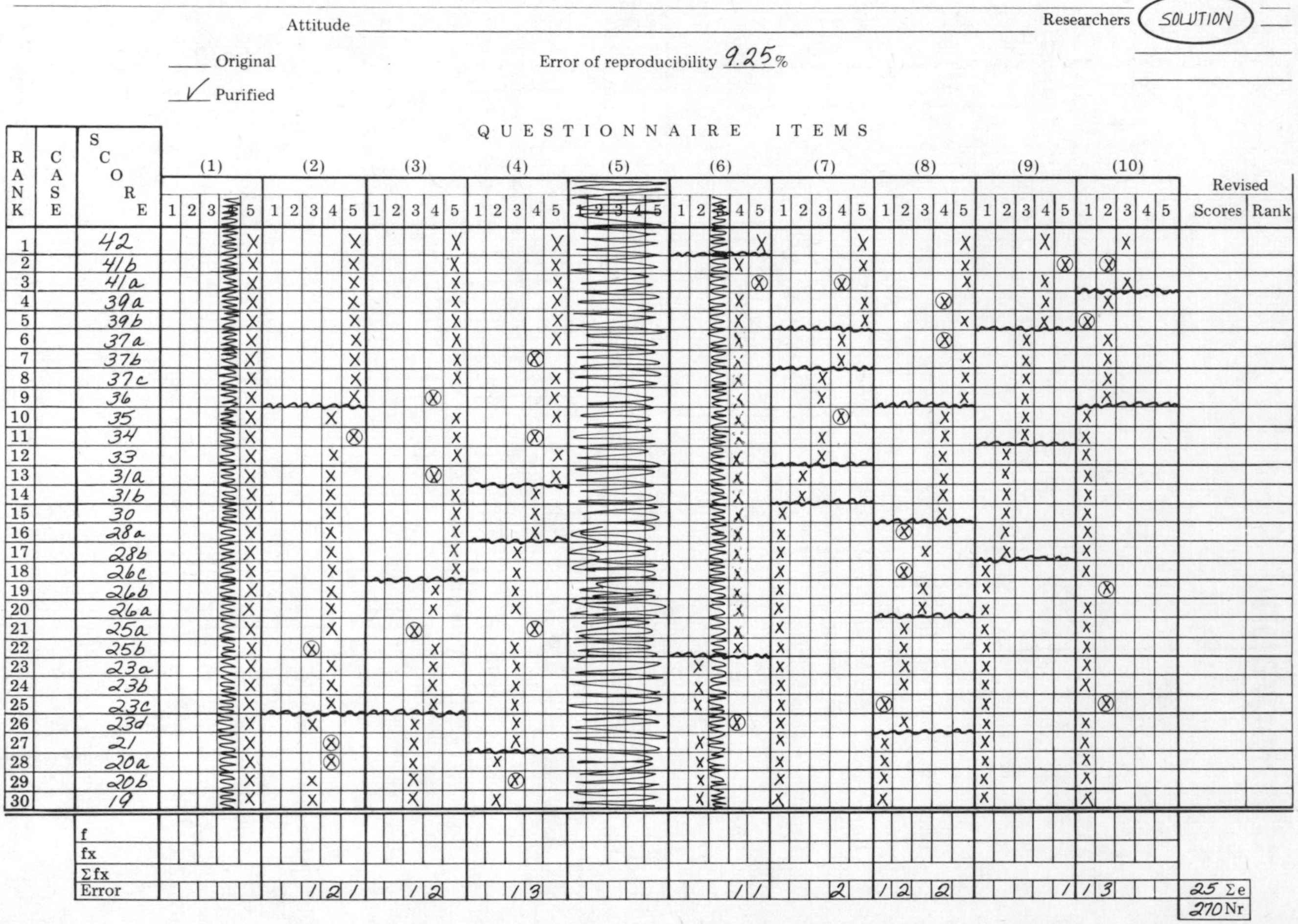

Bibliography

Bogardus, Emory S. *Immigration and Race Attitudes.* Boston: Heath, 1929.

———. *Social Distance.* Yellow Springs, Ohio: Antioch Press, 1959.

Bonjean, Charles M. *et al. Sociological Measurement: An Inventory of Scales and Indices.* San Francisco: Chandler Publishing Co., 1967.

Brinton, James E. "Deriving an Attitude Scale from Semantic Differential Data." *Public Opinion Quarterly* 25 (1961): 289-95.

Buchanan, William. *Understanding Political Variables.* New York: Charles Scribner's Sons, 1969.

Burgess, Ernest W., and Wallin, Paul. *Engagement and Marriage.* Philadelphia: J. B. Lippincott Co., 1953.

Champion, Dean J. *Basic Statistics for Social Research.* Scranton, Pa.: Chandler Publishing Co., 1970.

Dell Orto, A. E. *A Guttman Facet Analysis of the Racial Attitudes of Rehabilitation Counselor Trainees.* Unpublished doctoral dissertation, Michigan State University, 1970.

Dodd, Stuart C. "A Social Distance Test in the Near East." *American Journal of Sociology* 41 (September, 1935): 194-204.

Duijker, H. C. J. "Comparative Research in Social Science with Special Reference to Attitude Research." *International Social Science Bulletin* 7 (1955): 555-66.

Dynes, Russell R. "Church-Sect Typology and Socio-Economic Status." *American Sociological Review* 20 (October, 1955): 555-60.

Erb, D. L. *Racial Attitudes and Empathy: A Guttman Facet Theory Examination of their Relationships and Determinants.* Unpublished doctoral dissertation, Michigan State University, 1969.

Felty, J. E. "The Measurement of Attitudes Toward Disability in San Jose, Costa Rica. A Scale Approach to the Problem of Concept Equivalence." *Proceedings of the IX Inter-American Congress of Psychology*, Miami, Fla. (December, 1964), pp. 715-21.

Foa, U. G. "A Facet Approach to the Prediction of Commonalities." *Behavioral Science* 8 (1963): 220-26.

Goode, William J., and Hatt, Paul K. *Methods in Social Research*. New York: McGraw-Hill Book Co., 1952.

Gorden, Raymond L. "Interaction Between Attitude and the Definition of the Situation in the Expression of Opinion." *American Sociological Review* 17, No. 1 (1952): 50–58.

———. *Interviewing: Strategy, Techniques and Tactics*. Homewood, Ill.: Dorsey Press, 1975.

Green, Bert F. "Attitude Measurement." In Gardner Lindzey (ed.), *Theory and Method*, Vol. 1 in *Handbook of Social Psychology*. Reading, Mass.: Addison-Wesley Publishing Co., 1954.

Guttman, Louis L. "The Basis for Scalogram Analysis." In G. M. Maranell (ed.), *Scaling: A Sourcebook for Behavioral Scientists*. Chicago: Aldine Publishing Co., 1974.

———. "The Development of Nonmetric Space Analysis: A letter to Professor John Ross." *Multivariate Behavioral Research* 2 (1967): 71–82.

———. "Introduction to Facet Design and Analysis." In *Proceedings of the Fifteenth Congress of Sociology, Brussels, 1957*.

———. "Order Analysis of Correlation Matrices." In R. B. Cattell (ed.), *Handbook of Multivariate Experimental Psychology*. Chicago: Rand McNally, 1966.

———. "The Principal Components of Scalable Attitudes." In Paul F. Lazarsfeld (ed.), *Mathematical Thinking in the Social Sciences*. Glencoe, Ill.: The Free Press, 1954.

———. "The Problem of Attitude and Opinion Measurement." In S. A. Stauffer (ed.), *Measurement and Prediction*. Princeton: Princeton University Press, 1950.

———. "A Structural Theory for Intergroup Beliefs and Action." *American Sociological Review* 24, No. 3 (June, 1959): 318–28.

———., and Schlesinger, I. M. "The Analysis of Diagnostic Effectiveness of a Facet Theory Designed Battery of Achievement and Analytical Tests." The Israel Institute of Applied Social Research, Jerusalem, Israel. United States Department of Health, Education, and Welfare, OE-5-21-006, 1967.

Jordan, J. E. "A Guttman Facet Theory Analysis of Teacher Attitudes Toward the Mentally Retarded in Colombia, British Honduras, and the United States." *Indian Journal of Mental Retardation* 3 (1970): 1–20.

Kaiser, H. F. "Scaling a Simplex." *Psychometrika* 27 (1962): 155–66.

Kerlinger, F. N. "Progressiveness and Traditionalism: Basic Factors of Educational Attitudes." *Journal of Social Psychology* 48 (1958): 111–35.

Likert, Rensis. "A Technique for the Measurement of Attitudes." *Archives of Psychology* 140 (1932): 55.

Lingoes, J. C. "An IBM-7090 Program for Guttman-Lingoes Smallest Space Analysis-I." *Behavioral Science* 10 (1965): 183–84.

Maranell, Gary M. (ed.) *Scaling: A Sourcebook for Behavioral Scientists*. Chicago: Aldine Publishing Co., 1974.

McRae, Duncan, Jr. *Dimensions of Congressional Voting*. Berkeley: University of California Press, 1958.

Miller, Delbert C. *Handbook of Research Design and Social Measurement.* New York: David McKay Co., 1964.

Murphy, Gardner, and Likert, Rensis. *Public Opinion and the Individual.* New York: Harper, 1938.

Nie, Norman H.; Bent, Dale H.; and Hull, Hadlai. *Statistical Package for the Social Sciences.* New York: McGraw-Hill Book Co., 1970.

Orto, A. E. Bell. *A Guttman Facet Analysis of the Racial Attitudes of Rehabilitation Counselor Trainees.* Unpublished doctoral dissertation, Michigan State University, 1970.

Osgood, Charles E.; Suci, George J.; and Tannenbaum, Percy H. *The Measurement of Meaning.* Urbana, Ill.: University of Illinois Press, 1957.

Park, Robert E. "The Concept of Social Distance." *Journal of Applied Sociology* 8 (1902): 339–44.

Pope, Liston. *Millhands and Preachers.* New Haven: Yale University Press, 1942.

Schubert, Glendon. *Quantitative Analysis of Judicial Behavior.* Glencoe, Ill.: The Free Press, 1959.

Smith, D. H., and Inkeles, Alex. "The OM Scale: A Comparative Socio-Psychological Measure of Individual Modernity." *Sociometry* 29, No. 4 (December, 1966): 353–77.

Smith, Joel. "A Method for the Classification of Areas on the Basis of Demographically Homogeneous Populations." *American Sociological Review* 19 (April, 1954): 201–207.

Stouffer, Samuel A. *et al. Measurement and Prediction*, Vol. 4 in *Studies in Social Psychology in World War II.* Princeton: Princeton University Press, 1950.

Suchman, Edward A. "The Utility of Scalogram Analysis." In Samuel A. Stouffer *et al., Measurement and Prediction*, Vol. 4 in *Studies in Social Psychology in World War II.* Princeton: Princeton University Press, 1950.

Thurstone, Louis L., and Chave, E. J. *The Measurement of Attitudes.* Chicago: University of Chicago Press, 1929.

Torgerson, Warren S. *Theory and Methods of Scaling.* New York: John Wiley & Sons, Inc., 1958.

Wallin, Paul. "A Guttman Scale for Measuring Women's Neighborliness." *American Journal of Sociology* 59 (1953): 243–46.

von Wiese, Leopold, and Becker, Howard. *Systematic Sociology.* John Wiley & Sons, Inc., 1932.

White, Benjamin W., and Saltz, Eli. "Measurement of Reproducibility." In Gary M. Maranell (ed.), *Scaling: A Sourcebook for Behavioral Scientists.* Chicago: Aldine Publishing Co., 1974.

Wolf, R. M. "Construction of Descriptive and Attitude Scales." In T. Husen (ed.), *International Study of Achievement in Mathematics.* New York: John Wiley & Sons, Inc., 1967.

Zinnes, J. L. "Scaling." In P. H. Mussen and M. R. Rosenzweig (eds.), *Annual Review of Psychology*, Vol. 20 (1969), pp. 447–78.

Index